CURRENT AFRICAN ISSUES 63

Agricultural Water Institutions in East Africa

Edited by: Atakilte Beyene

NORDISKA AFRIKAINSTITUTET, UPPSALA 2015

INDEXING TERMS:
Water resources
Water management
Irrigation systems
Climate change
Agriculture
Farming
Community participation
Appropriate technology
Development projects
Case studies
Kenya
Tanzania

The opinions expressed in this volume are those of the authors
and do not necessarily reflect the views of the Nordic Africa Institute.

ISSN 0280-2171
ISBN 978-91-7106-777-7
© The authors, The Nordic Africa Institute.
Cover photo: A Somali elder cleans his face in an irrigation canal, 40 km North of Beledweyne, Somalia. By Ilyas A Abukar. Public Domain
Production: Byrå4
Print on demand, Lightning Source UK Ltd.

Contents

Short biographies of authors 5

Acrimony 8

1. Introduction 9
   Agricultural water resources in perspective 9
   Key aspects of water institution reforms 10
   The case studies 16
   References 18

2. Performance Assessment and Evaluation of Community Participation in Water
   Sector Governance 23
   The case of Ngaciuma-Kinyaritha catchment, Mount Kenya Region 23
   Introduction 23
   Purpose of the study 24
   Literature review 25
   Methodology 27
   Results and discussion 29
   Conclusion and recommendations 36
   Key policies and research implications 37
   References 38

3. Climate Change, Pro-Poor Schemes and Water Inequality 43
   Strengths and Weaknesses of Kauti Irrigation Water Users' Association, Kenya ... 43
   Introduction 43
   Purpose of the Study 44
   Literature Review 44
   Methodology 46
   Results and Discussion 49
   Conclusion and Recommendations 55
   Key Policies and Research Implications 55
   References 56

4. Competitive Farming Strategies and their Effect on Water Provision and
   Profitability among Smallholder Farms 61
   The Case of Muooni Dam Site, Kenya 61
   Introduction 61
   Purpose of the Study 62
   Review of the Field 62
   Methodology 64
   Results and Discussion 68
   Conclusion and Recommendations 71
   Key Policies and Research Implications 72
   References 73

5. Strengthening Formal Institutions in the Lake Victoria Basin: Role of Integrated Icts in Sustainable Irrigation Resources 77
Introduction 77
Purpose 77
Overview of Irrigation Water Resources 78
Research Questions 84
Methodology 84
Results and Discussions 87
Conclusions and Suggestion for Future Studies 94
Key Policy and Research Implications 94
Acknowledgements 95
References 95

Short biographies of authors

Akombo, Rose Adhiambo (MSc) is an Assistant Director at the Kenya Forest Service, where she manages the Climate Change Response Programme. She is currently a PhD candidate at the Department of Geography of Kenyatta University. Her research expertise encompasses a large array of field assessment on forestry and forest hydrology with climate change adaptation and mitigation initiatives, especially REDD+ mechanism.

Bader, O. Essam (Prof.) is an Associate Professor of agricultural economics at the Damietta University (Damietta, Egypt), with a significant experience in research on water economics with a focus on irrigation optimization in Arid and Semi-Arid Lands (ASALs). He is also widely consulted by the German Academic Exchange Program (DAAD) and the German Water Alumni Network (GAWN).

Beyene, Atakilte (PhD) is a senior researcher at the Nordic Africa Institute. He holds a PhD in development studies from the Swedish University of Agricultural Sciences and has worked in universities and research institutes in Sweden and Ethiopia. His research focuses on agrarian and rural institutions, natural resource management, food security and gender. He has conducted extensive field studies in Ethiopia and Tanzania. He has coordinated interdisciplinary research projects in Nordic and African countries. His current research includes large-scale agricultural investments in Africa and their implications for local economies.

Doke, Dzigbodi Adzo (PhD) is a Lecturer at the Department of Environment and Resource Studies of the University for Development Studies, Ghana. Her main focus is in risk assessment of key environmental factors. She is the recipient of several awards including a Fulbright and is widely consulted for providing technical advice on environmental management issues in the northern sector of Ghana.

Kinuthia, Wanja (PhD) is a Senior Researcher for tropical insects at the Department of Zoology of the National Museums of Kenya and has headed the Department of Invertebrate Zoology. She consults on suitable crops and tree species for sustainable agricultural water management for food and nutritional security. She is also a student mentor and champions the best practices for pollinator conservation.

Luwesi, Cush Ngonzo (PhD) is currently the Focal Region Manager of the CGIAR Research Program on Water, Land and Ecosystems (WLE) for the Volta and Niger basins. He was the 2014 best scholar at Kenyatta University (Nairobi, Kenya) for his multidisciplinary contributions to economic evaluation of watershed resources under changing climate patterns and interventions. He also spearheads the African wing of geoengineering initiative by Harvard University (US) and several German universities.

Mongi, Hector (Mr.) is a researcher at the interface between natural resource management and Information and Communication Technologies (ICTs). He is specifically interested in climate change adaptation for the water sector, ICT user research and technologies for citizen engagement. Currently he is Lecturer at the Department of Information Systems, the University of Dodoma, Tanzania. He is also a PhD scholar at the same Department.

Mutiso, Mary Nyawira (MA) has over 20 years in teaching and research. She is an assistant lecturer of development and economic geography at the Department of Community Development at South Eastern Kenya University and PhD candidate at the Department of Geography of Kenyatta University. Her research deals with the nexus between poverty and natural resource management. She is also a devoted discussant of the geoengineering initiative by American and German universities.

Mvuma, Aloys (Prof.) is an experienced researcher in systems engineering, computer information systems and electrical engineering. Currently is Associate Professor at the Department of Telecommunications and Communications Networks of the University of Dodoma. He is also serving as Principal of College of Informatics and Virtual Education at the same University.

Ngamba, Jean-Filston Mikwa (MSc) is an assistant lecturer of Land Resource Management at the Faculty of Agronomy of the University of Kisangani (DR Congo), where he is currently pursuing a PhD degree. His research focus on spatial models for forest resource mapping and irrigation suitability assessment under changing soil and forestry patterns.

Obando, Joy Apiyo (Prof.) is an Associate Professor of Geography at the Department of Geography of Kenyatta University specializing in geomorphology and Integrated Watershed Management (IWM). She works as an interface between physical geography and management in a watershed .She was Director at the Financial Aid office at Kenyatta University five years and coordinated the IWMNet/ EU Project. She is also widely the German Academic Exchange Program (DAAD), She was a cluster leader for the Lake Victoria Research Initiative (VICRES) and Principal Investigator for the UPGRO Catalyst Grant.

Ruhakana, Albert (MSc) is a researcher at the Department of Natural Resource Management, of the Rwanda Agriculture Board, where he coordinates soil and water management projects. He holds degree in Integrated Watershed Management with substantial post graduate credentials in advanced technologies, GIS and remote sensing applied to watershed management.

Wambua, Peter Philip (PhD) is a lecturer of Human Resource Management in the Department of Business Administration of Kenyatta University. His research interests cut across the disciplines of Human Resource, Strategic Management, Marketing and Entrepreneurship. He is accredited with a significant number of publications focusing on performance evaluation of teaching service delivery, performance contracting and curriculum development in public universities in Kenya using a business perspective. He was awarded the best lecturer award in 2014 by the management of Kenyatta University due to his contributions in teaching, research and community service.

AEZ	Agro-Ecological Zones
ASAL	Arid and Semi-Arid Lands
BWS	Blue Water Saving
CAAC	Catchment Areas Advisory Committees
CDM	Clean Development Mechanisms
CMS	Catchment Management Strategy
CWMS	Community Water Management Systems
EMCA	Environmental Management Coordination Act
ENSO	El Niño Southern Oscillation
ES	Ecological/Environmental Services
EWS	Early Warning Systems
FGD	Focus Group Discussion
GoK	Government of Kenya
GWC	Green Water Credits
GWS	Green Water Saving
LIF	Legal and Institutional Framework
LSCA	Lower Sub-Catchment Area
PAE	Performance Assessment and Evaluation
PES	Payments for Ecological/Environmental Services
PPF	Production Possibility Frontiers
PPP	Public-Private Partnerships
PWS	Payment for Watershed Services
REDD+	Reducing Emissions from Deforestation and forest Degradation
SCMP	Sub-Catchment Management Plans
SPSS	Statistical Package for Social Sciences
SWC	Soil and Water Conservation
USCA	Upper Sub-Catchment Area
WAB	Water Appeal Boards
WASREB	Water Services Regulatory Board
WRMA	Water Resources Management Authority
WRMD	Water Resource Management and Development
WRUA	Water Resource Users' Associations
WSB	Water Services' Boards
WSP	Water Service Providers

1. Introduction

Atakilte Beyene

Agricultural water resources in perspective

Many countries in East Africa are introducing new water policies and reforming existing ones (e.g., Laube 2007; Schwartz 2008). Water reforms that concern the agricultural sector are by far the most significant in terms of the scale and volume of water resources. This is not only because agriculture is the major user of water (accounting for about 70% of all current fresh water withdrawals globally and over 90% in most of the world's least-developed countries) (WWAP 2014), but also because it faces unprecedented challenges that require major efforts in order to ensure its sustainability. First, Africa's food production system is dominantly rain-fed. Increasingly, dependency on rainfall has become a major source of insecurity in food production across the continent. According to the IPCC (Intergovernmental Panel on Climate Change) report, climate change is causing an increased incidence of drought, and growing variability and uncertainty in rainfall, and these changes are putting Africa's food security and survival at risk (IPCC 2012). In Kenya, for instance, the combined economic impacts of recurrent drought and related shocks is estimated to cost the economy 0,7–1,0 percent of the GDP (Demombynes and Kiringai 2011). A recent report by the International food policy research Institute (IFPRI) indicates that climate change is a major factor in water conflicts in sub-Saharan Africa (SSA) (Priscoli and Wolf 2009, IFPRI 2015). Minimising these risks is a priority for the continent and there is a sense of urgency in improving the provision, security and utilisation of water resources for food, feed and fibre and other products (CAADP 2003).

Second, global pressure on and competition for water is also rapidly growing across the SSA region. Since the late 2000s, regional and global food and energy demands and insecurity have increased dramatically. Following the food and oil crisis of 2008, the proportion of land and water resources that have been transferred to investors, both foreign and domestic, for commercial farming has increased dramatically (Land Matrix 2015). In these transfers, water is the key resource that attracts investors (Mehta, Velderisch and Franco 2012; Woodhouse and Ganho 2011). A recent study indicates that the volume of water transferred in these large-scale land deals is equivalent to the volume of water that would be required to address the food insecurity of, and malnutrition in, the countries that are hosting the investments (Rulli, Saviori and D'Odorica 2013). The pattern observed is that the land allocations take place in areas where water is available, mainly along rivers and lake basins. Construction of large-scale dams is also booming in parts of Africa, as in the case of the Nile and Lake Victoria Basins. These dams are often multipurpose and aim at the expansion of various economic activities such as energy (hydropower), fisheries, transport and tourism. These emerging water demands are likely to create challenges for water-use allocation decisions and in managing the risk of conflict and inequalities in access to and use of water at local and regional levels.

Finally, Africa's demographic, urban and income expansions are also expected to accelerate demand for irrigated produce. Africa is among the fast urbanising regions, and by 2035 almost 53% of the population (from the current 40%) is expected to live in urban areas (FAO/UNIDO 2010). Anticipated growth in incomes and the size of the middle class in urban areas will result in demand for irrigated products, such as vegetables and fruits. Some analysts have estimated that 60% of added food required will come from irrigation (Plusquellec 2002) and by 2050, agriculture will need to produce 100% more in developing countries (WWAP 2015). As these products are water-intensive, their production places high pressure on water resources. The market and political forces that emerge in response to demographic and consumption changes are expected to cause significant change in the allocation of water resources from rural and environmental sectors to urban and industry sectors.

These broad and interlinked processes are creating a growing sense of urgency about reforming agricultural water sectors in two respects: improving availability and supply of water, and setting up water institutions. On the water supply side, many regional development organisations (e.g., CAADP 2003; AGRA 2014) have recently proposed significant increases in investments in water infrastructure, such as dams and irrigation canals, across Africa. Related to these are the promotion of watershed and catchment rehabilitation and protection in order to reduce siltation in dams and canals. These new water schemes are necessitating the reconfiguration or creation of new institutions and organisations in order to create or improve water management systems that address access to and distribution and use of water resources. This issue paper focuses on the latter aspect, namely, institutional and organisational reform. The case studies from East Africa presented in chapters 2 to 5 address some of the key institutional and organisational aspects of water.

Key aspects of water institution reforms

In this introductory section, three major issues are extrapolated from the case studies and the literature to highlight three the key issues facing the reforms being introduced in the region. These are:

1. Informal water institutions and the quest to formalise them
2. Sustainability of ecosystem services, and
3. Coordination of institutions and information systems across stakeholders

Introduction

Informal water institutions and the quest for formalisation

One of the major features of current water reforms is that they invariably tend to pursue formalisation of water institutions as part of the development agenda. In fact, the very notion of water reform departs from the general assumption that state policies and laws will institute new institutions and organisations to manage water resources. This is particularly evident in irrigation schemes, where public and non-governmental organisations are involved in financing, operating and organising the schemes. Progress in formalisation, however, is not guaranteed. As the results of this study indicate, the outcomes are mixed. Instead of effecting a smooth institutional transition, the process is characterised by selective inclusion and exclusion of actors, conflicts and the persistence of multiple institutional setups.

It is well recognised that access to and use of irrigation water in rural Africa involves informal and formal institutions (Meinzen-Dick and Nkonya 2007). The informal institutions are widely distributed across the continent and are highly localised and context-specific. For instance, small-scale irrigation schemes, rural livestock farming and small-scale fishery systems generally rely on informal institutions. These latter evolve in response to prevailing social and economic situations and are embedded in the customs, traditions and beliefs of the local people (Ostrom 2005). Informal institutions tend to prevail at the local and grassroots level of water management (ibid).

While there is growing acceptance of informal institutions in small-scale and fragmented water-use systems, there is also recognition of the need to formalise them, particularly where competition for water is high or new schemes are introduced (Garces-Restrepo et al. 2007). In irrigation schemes, for instance, transfers of management to local people seek to formalise water institutions and water organisations. This is often justified by the need to impose water fees as a means to recover investment costs and recurrent operation and maintenance costs. There is also another, more fundamental, argument in favour of formalisation stemming from claims that many informal water institutions embody unregulated access to water and inefficient water use (Easter, Rosegrant and Dinar 1999). The shortcomings of the informal sectors include difficulty in achieving incentive structures, high transaction costs and weak mechanisms for investment in the development and management of water resources (Saleth and Dinar 2004). Where informal institutions dominate, access to and accumulation of resources is embedded in social relationships in which kinship, marriage, client networks and circles of trading friends are important factors (Clough 2014).

Formalisation of water institutions refers to the extent to which access, use and management of water resources comes under the direct legal and regulatory influence of the state (Angueletou-Marteau 2008). In contrast to the informal institutions, formal institutions "stress the importance of state-level institutions to the expansion of a homogenous impersonal market" (Clough 2014: xvii). Meinzen-Dick distinguishes three alternative approaches to developing irrigation institutions: by states, markets or users (Meinzen-Dick 2007). Government and non-governmental organisation intervention in financing and delivering water infrastructure is often seen as positive in water development (Briceño-Garmendia, Smits and Foster 2008), but reliance on bureaucratic administration and management systems generally entails the risk of failure and mismanagement of water resources (Mukherji et al. 2009). The market mechanism to regulate water resources, especially in the provision and delivery services of water, emphasises economic and financial issues and the role of the market in water rights allocations (e.g., Pattanayak, Wunder and Ferraro 2010, Tsur et al. 2004). This, however, is controversial and difficult to implement. The failure of markets to capture externalities in water uses, in general, and the lack of other institutional conditions such as regulatory enforcement in developing countries, in particular, are arguments against market mechanisms for water (e.g., Redford and Adams 2009). In addition, there is a moral aspect: water is a basic resource that humans must have access to and should be under public management (e.g., Calaguas 1999). Thus, privatisation and commodification of water as potential alternative mechanisms for water management in developing countries face uncertainty. The user perspective of water highlights the role of local institutions and organisations in water use. The literature on the level, scope and dynamics of local institutions and organisations in managing water resources is overwhelming, especially in developing countries (e.g., Hagedorn 2013, Callejo and Cossio 2009, Bruns 2007, Garces-Restrepo, Vermillion and Munoz 2007, Saleth and Dinar 2004). Concepts such as Common Pool Resources, Water User Associations, Traditional User Systems, Community Management Systems, etc. are embedded in the user perspective (Ostrom 1990, 2005).

The distinctions made above are largely analytical. In reality, elements of all the three approaches are exercised by different actors in the same location, although the relative significance of each aspect can vary significantly. For instance, in irrigation schemes state-driven water institutions and local water user institutions may operate simultaneously and "coexist." In other cases, small-scale water providers, operating very much along market lines, are active in urban and rural water provision (South Africa and Botswana). Thus, institutional pluralism in irrigation systems is a reality in many countries in Africa.

Consequently, current reforms can benefit from research that addresses the coexistence and interface of multiple institutions. Such coexistence is not without competition and conflict. Differences in power relations and the emergence of new agricultural market opportunities for rural people can generate friction and restructure local institutional and organisational arrangements for water (see Chapter 2). Creating shared responsibility for water management among different actors and institutions in a constructive and collaborative decision-making process is identified as a key challenge facing water reforms. In striking the right balance between state, private and community activities, legal and institutional environments is thus crucial in water management.

The push for formalisation from above (administrative or market mechanisms) is also influenced by local social and economic dynamics. An important observation in this regard is that some local interest groups reinforce the formalisation processes. For instance, differentiation of local people in terms of their capacity, market relations and endowments reveals how local individuals behave and how groups are formed. Well positioned and powerful groups among local people are increasingly aligned with the formalisation processes being promoted by governments. As will be elaborated in Chapter 4, well-off and commercially well-connected local farmers support a more exclusionary institutional arrangement for water access and use.

Finally, poverty is an important issue that needs to be raised in formalisation processes. In a context where poverty is still a major challenge and alternative livelihoods are limited, the question of inclusiveness stands out as a critical challenge for formalisation. As will be elaborated in Chapter 2, the dilemma is that the very notion of formalisation involves defining individuals or users as legitimate entities and as having exclusive rights to use the water resources. This implies delineating social boundaries in terms of users and non-users.

Mechanisms to secure ecosystem services

The challenge of distributing consequences and benefits from any human intervention in natural resources, water systems in particular, is well recognised (Buscher 2008, Redford and Adams 2009). Water flows and interconnects users at different places. This implies that externalities generated by a user in one place affect another user located elsewhere (Engel, Pagiola and Wunder 2008). One well-known challenge in irrigation schemes is the lack of integration between upstream and downstream management systems. Discussion of sustainability of irrigation schemes often focuses on the built infrastructure, typically management of canal systems. Hence, mechanisms to recover costs of dams and canals, and to enforce water fees to cover operation and maintenance systems, are the focus of most irrigation schemes.

Yet sustainable irrigation systems are highly dependent on broader ecosystem services upstream. Irrigation schemes often require clean and abundant water. This in turn requires healthy watersheds and ecosystems, involving complex interactions of soil, water, vegetation and climate. Establishing mechanisms that sustain such conditions is a policy priority. Ecosystem services (ES), defined as "the benefits people obtain from ecosystems" (MEA 2005), are vital to the regeneration of clean water and the decomposing of wastes.[1] Typically, protection of forest and vegetation and promotion of sustainable land use systems, including soil and water conservation, among upstream land users are seen as important for the sustainability of water supplies for irrigation schemes.

There is much discussion in watershed management and conservation about quantifying and paying for the services to societies that nature performs – labelled as Payments for Ecological/ Environmental Services (PES) (e.g., Wunder 2005; Gomez-Baggethun and Perez 2011; Kosoy and Corbera 2010; Peterson et al. 2010). PES schemes have been defined as "a voluntary transaction in which a well-defined ecosystem service is 'bought' by a minimum of one ecosystem buyer from a minimum of one ecosystem service provider if, and only if, ecosystem service provision is secured (conditionality)" (Wunder 2008).

Payments for watershed services have been recently tried in developing countries, mainly in Latin America but less often in Africa (Stanton et al. 2010). However, their feasibility is not well established. Based on a review of 95 payments for watershed services (PWS), Porras, Grieg-Gran and Veves (2008) identify challenges in operationalising payments, mainly due to the complexity of measuring and attributing changes in the provision of watershed services. Such schemes often depend on external funding, and the self-financing promise of PES is weak (Ferraro 2009). In other cases, lack of clear tenure and property ownership of land and water resources undermines PES mechanisms (Bruce, Wendland and Naughton-Treves 2010).

The major criticism of PES is its reliance on the market. In this vein, Gomez-Baggethun and Perez (2011) argue that PES is essentially a form of "commodification of ecosystem services with potential counterproductive effects for biodiversity conservation and equity of access to ecosystems benefits" (p. 1). The authors further argue that commodification has the political aspect of appropriation-dispossession and potentially creates conflicts in the distribution of ecological services (Gomez-Baggethun and Perez 2011). These risks are particularly high in less developed countries, for various reasons. In many African countries, market institutions and related capacities are weak. As Ferraro (2009) indicates, such schemes are heavily NGO-supported and not self-sustaining. Second, watershed management activities are predominantly part of national natural resource conservation programmes. Promotion of soil and water conservation, tree planting programmes and improved land use programmes (such as agroforestry) continue to be supported by governments and donors. Third, watershed areas continue to be covered by a mosaic of land use systems in which community ownership, open access and individual user-right systems coexist.

---

1. The four broad ES categories are: provisioning, such as production of water; regulating, such as control of disease; supporting, such as crop pollination; and cultural, such as spiritual benefits (MEA 2005).

In such contexts, the PES actors (buyers and sellers) are not easy to organise (Stanton et.al. 2010) and, hence, implementing PES through voluntary and market-based systems is simply not feasible. Finally, PES's contribution to poverty reduction and livelihood improvement is not clear and there is concern that the ability of poorer households to participate in PES schemes is not promising. Based on 287 case studies, Landell-Mills and Porras argue that market-based environmental services are unlikely to contribute to poverty reduction. In other cases, poorer households are less likely to have secure tenure and access to credit, and less likely to receive technical assistance (Landell-Mills and Porras 2002). The sustainability of financing watershed services depends on whether they are driven by water users, for example downstream irrigators. This largely depends on whether their production is profitable enough to generate the money needed to pay upstream services.

Taking all this into account, current policy reforms need to focus on promoting broad-based and pro-poor management systems. In Uganda, for instance, introduction of pro-poor water tariffs and special water projects targeting the poor have resulted in significant expansion of services (Kariuki et al. 2014). Unlike the above alternatives, this approach adopts a broader perspective. Daw et al. (2011) argue that instead of conceiving ES in terms of profiteering, broader objectives of poverty alleviation need to be emphasised. The authors suggest that different groups derive different benefits from ES. Stakeholder analysis and equity analysis can enhance the sustainable management of resources. Poverty-oriented water interventions thus need to be seen in terms of improved health, reduced health costs, increased productivity and time-savings. Progress in these is likely to build up sustainable livelihoods and improve the capacity of local people to rehabilitate degraded lands and better manage their resources.

Given the communal nature of tenure and access systems in many African watershed systems, community-based watershed management as the guiding principle for rehabilitating rural natural resources still appears to be practical and feasible. Improving resource management also requires addressing water-access inequalities and improving participation by local people. As Chapter 3 notes, strengthening competent local organisations, mobilising public resources, and decentralising institutions to allow for more participation by local people are critical issues that need to be considered.

Coordination and information in water management

In conditions where water management is the responsibility of many decision-makers in the public, private and community spheres, coordination of institutions and organisations is key (e.g., Timmerman 2015). Furthermore, irrigation systems typically display the spatial dimensions of water, creating needs for coordination. For instance, irrigation systems that use river or dam systems involve individuals, groups of users and even different communities pursuing different irrigation practices. In large-scale irrigation schemes, in particular, coordination is often provided by the state.

Beyond the need for coordinating institutions, information management and dissemination are becoming increasingly critical, especially in medium- and large-scale irrigation systems, where the number of people involved is large. Rapidly changing technologies mean that Africa can make good use of the technological revolution. As Chapter 5 discusses, information and communication technology (ICT) applications are playing an important role in connecting water users and water managers located in different organisational and geographic positions.

Given the continuing importance of community-based management of water resources, the question of how ICT opportunities can be integrated into local-regional management systems and the kinds of information and data that can be generated is critical. ICT has the potential to improve participation of water users and recognition of local context. As Ebi and Semenza (2008) indicate, coordinated community action is a necessary condition for adaptation to climate change. Community-based risk and vulnerability assessment for climate change can be fostered through active community participation in collecting information that is relevant and meaningful to local people. ICT as a tool can play a key role in promoting both vertical and horizontal interactions.

ICT application and use in water management systems, especially community-based ones, is not without challenges. One problem is scaling-up the information from community-based approaches (Burton, Dickinson and Howard 2007). Organising, processing and disseminating the information require inputs from participants external to the community. Effective links between communities and authorities at higher levels are needed. The processes are often resource-intensive and their financing is often a challenge, as they are not included in water management systems and strategies. The risk of distortion or selective inclusion/exclusion of data and information may also dis/empower participants (Allen 2006).

In such cases, states have greater roles to play at higher spatial scales, where data and information on water availability, water forecasts, early warning systems, etc. become integral aspects of the management systems.

The case studies

Four case studies from East Africa are presented in the following sections. The first study (Chapter 2) explores performance assessment and evaluation of community participation in water sector governance in the Mount Kenya Region. It highlights that while community participation in water management is critical, its institutionalisation is complex. By focusing on Kenya's water reforms, which aimed at formalising water service provision, the chapter evaluates the policy reforms in terms of their inclusiveness. Exclusion of traditional or informal water users and limitations on community-wide stakeholder involvement are some of the key challenges such policy reforms encounter. Delineation of users and non-users, and performance evaluations as between formal and non-formal users appear not to have been well considered when the water reform was introduced. The authors argue that the reforms are often focused on water users downstream of catchment areas. Upstream stakeholders and the significance of payment for catchment management are not fully considered in the reforms.

The second case (Chapter 3) explores the pro-poor perspective in improving access to water in a context where climate change and water inequality prevail. In areas where water is scarce and climate change is a threat, building the capacities and skills of local water users, especially the marginalised and poor, are critical to ensuring access to water. In such conditions, there are incentives for introducing mechanisms that enhance efficient distribution and utilisation of water resources. Mechanisms such as Green Water Saving are promising, but financial support is needed for such initiatives to flourish.

The third case (Chapter 4) study examines effects of competitive farming, especially intensive irrigation schemes, on water demand. Competitive farming strategies in the Muooni Dam site in Kenya rely on both differentiation and diversification of crops to optimise water utilisation. These strategies, however, appear to cause excessive water abstraction from dams and river systems. The farmers pursue their maximising strategies without considering the available water. In order to discourage such behaviour, mechanisms that account for and balance individual water withdrawals and total or potential water availability at catchment or basin levels and that improve awareness among users, are important.

The final study (Chapter 5) explores the role of ICT (Information and Communication technologies) in improving participation by and coordination of stakeholders in irrigation and water-use management systems in the Lake Victoria Basin. The current dramatic advances in and expansion of ICT have improved access to information and communication in rural Africa. This technology has touched every aspect of life in rural and urban areas. However, integration of ICT into water systems and water infrastructure is in its infancy. This requires both horizontal and vertical integration of ICT. Horizontally, grassroots-level sharing of information can enhance participation by local users in the planning, management and maintenance of irrigation schemes. Vertical integration, on the other hand, can help to connect organisations both among themselves and with grassroots water users.

Each of the chapter provides a set of key policy and research implications and recommendations.

References

AGRA (Alliance for a Green Revolution in Africa) (2014) African agriculture status report: Climate change and smallholder agriculture in sub-Sahara Africa. Nairobi, Kenya.

Allen, K. (2006) "Community-based disaster preparedness and climate adaptation: Local capacity-building in Philippines." *Disaster* 30(1): 81–101.

Angueletou-Marteau, A. (2008) Informal water suppliers meeting water needs in the peri-urban territories of Mumbai, an Indian perspective. In: *Global changes and water resources: Confronting the expanding and diversifying pressures.* Montpellier, France: XIIIth World Water Congress. Available at http://halshs.archives-ouvertes.fr/docs/00/36/34/64/PDF/Angueletou_NT20-2008_.pdf

Briceño-Garmendia, C., K. Smits and V. Foster (2008) Financing infrastructure in Sub-Sahara Africa: Patterns and options. The International Bank for Reconstruction and Development, The World Bank, Washington DC.

Bruce, J., K. Wendland and L. Naughton-Treves (2010) Whom to pay? Key Concepts and Terms Regarding Tenure and Property Rights in Payment-Based Forest Ecosystem Conservation. Land Tenure Center Policy Brief 15. Available at http://www.nelson.wisc.edu/ltc/

Bruns, B. (2007), 'Irrigation water rights: options for pro-poor reform', *Irrigation and Drainage,* 56: 237–46.

Burton, I., T. Dickinson and Y. Howard (2007) "Integrating adaptation into policy: Upscaling evidence from local to global." *Climate Policy* 7(4): 371–6.

Buscher, B. (2008) Conservation, neoliberalism and social science: a critical reflection on SCB 2007 annual meeting in South Africa. *Conservation Biology,* 22 (2) 229–31.

CAADP (Comprehensive Africa Agriculture Development Program-about) (2014). Available at http://www.nepad.org/foodsecurity/agriculture/about.

Calaguas, B. (1999) The right to water, sanitation and hygiene and the human rights-based approach to development. Water Aid.

Callejo, I. and V. Cossio (2009) institutional aspects of sustainability for irrigated agriculture in arid and semiarid regions, *Chilean Journal of Agricultural Research,* 69 (1) 41–3.

Clough, P. (2014) *Morality and economic growth in rural West Africa: Indigenous accumulation in Hausaland.* New York: Berghahn.

Daw, T., K. Brown, S. Rosendo and R. Pomeroy (2011) "Applying the ecosystem services concept to poverty alleviation: The need to disaggregate human well-being." *Environmental Conservation* 38 (4) 370–9.

Demombynes, G. and J. Kiringai (2011) the drought and food crisis in the Horn of Africa: Impacts and proposed policy response for Kenya. Poverty Reduction and Economic Management Newtwork (PREM), Economic Premise, the World Bank. Available at http://siteresources.worldbank.org/INTPREMNET/Resources/EP71.pdf

Easter, K., M. Rosegrant and A. Dinar (1999) Formal and informal markets for water: Institutions, performance and constraints. The World Bank Research Observer, vol 14 (1) 99–116.

Ebi, K. and Semenza, J. (2008) Community-based adaptation to health impacts of climate change. American Journal of Preventive Medicine, 35 (5) 501–7.

Engel, S., S. Pagiola and S. Wunder (2008) Designing payments for environmental services in theory and practice – An overview of the issues. *Ecological Economics* 65:663–674.

FAO/UNIDO (2010) *African agribusiness and agro-industries development initiative (3ADI): A program framework*. Rome: Food and Agricultural Organisation.

Ferraro, P. (2009) Regional review of payments for watershed services: Sub-Saharan Africa. *Journal of Sustainable Forestry,* 28: 525–50.

Garces-Restrepo, C., D. Vermillion and G. Munoz (2007) *Irrigation management transfer: worldwide efforts and results*. Rome: Food and Agricultural Organisation.

Gomez-Baggethun, E. and M. Perez (2011) "Economic valuation and the commodification of ecosystem services." *Progress in Physical Geography* 35: 617–32.

Hagedorn, K. (2013) Natural resource management: the role of cooperative institutions and

IFPRI (International Food Policy Research Institute) (2015) *2014–2015 Global Food Policy Report*. Washington DC: International Food Policy Research Institute.

IFPRI (International Food Policy Research Institute) (2015) 2014–2015 Global Food Policy Report. Washington, DC: International Food Policy Research Institute.

IPCC (2012) Managing the risks of extreme events and disaster to advance climate change adaptation. A special report of the Intergovernmental Panel on Climate Change (IPCC). Available at: https://www.ipcc.ch/pdf/special-reports/srex/SREX_Full_Report.pdf

Kariuki, M., G. Patricot, R. Rop, S. Mutono and M. Makino (2014) Do pro-poor policies increase water coverage? : an analysis of service delivery in Kampala's informal settlements. Washington DC, World Bank Group. Available at http://documents.worldbank.org/curated/en/2014/01/19101493/pro-poor-policies-increase-water-coverage-analysis-service-delivery-kampalas-informal-settlements

Kosoy, N. and E. Corbera (2010) "Payment for ecosystem services as commodity fetishism." *Ecological Economics* 69(6) 1228–36.

Land Matrix (2014). The Online Public Database on Land Deals. Available at http://www.landmatrix.org/en/ accessed on 18 March 2015.

Landell-Mills, N. and I. Porras (2002) *Silver bullet or fools' gold? A global review of markets for forest environmental services and their impact on the poor. Instruments for sustainable private sector forestry series.* London: International Institute for Environment and Development.

Laube, W. (2007) "The promise and perils of water reforms: Perspectives from northern Ghana." *Afrika Spectrum* 42(3): 419–37.

MEA (Millennium Ecosystem Assessment) (2005) Ecosystems and human well-being: Synthesis. Island Press, Washington, DC.

Mehta, L., G. Velderisch and J. Franco (2012) "Introduction to the special issue: Water Grabbing? Focus on the (Re)appropriation of Finite Water Resources." *Water Alternatives* 5(2): 193–207.

Meinzen-Dick, R. and L. Nkonya (2007) "Understanding legal pluralism in water and land rights: Lessons from Africa and Asia." In B. van Koppen, M. Giordano, J. Butterworth (eds) *Community-based Water Law and Water Resources Management Reform in Developing Countries: Comprehensive Assessment of Water Management in Agriculture, Series 5.* Wallingford: CAB International, pp. 12–27.

Mukherji, A.; T. Facon, J. Burke, C. de Fraiture, J. Faures, B. Fuleki, M. Giordano, D. Molden, and T. Shah (2009) Revitalizing Asia's irrigation: To sustainably meet tomorrow's food needs. Colombo: IWMI and Rome: FAO.

Ostrom, E (2005) *Understanding Institutional Diversity.* Princeton and Oxford: Princeton University Press.

Ostrom, E. (1990) Governing the commons: The evolution of institutions for collective action. New York: Cambridge University Press.

Ostrom, E. (2005) Understanding Institutional Diversity. Princeton, NJ: Princeton University Press.

Pattanayak, S., S. Wunder and P. Ferraro (2010) Show me the money: do payments supply environmental services in developing countries? *Review of Environmental Economics and Policy, 4, 254–74.*

Peterson, M., D. Hall, A. Feldpausch-Parker and T. Peterson (2010) "Obscuring Ecosystem Function with Application of the Ecosystem Services Concept." *Conservation Biology* 24(1): 113–19.

Plusquellec, H. (2002) Is the daunting challenge of irrigation achievable? *Irrigation and Drainage* 51(3) 185–98.

Porras, I., M. Grieg-Gran and N. Veves (2008) All that glitters: A review of payments for watershed services in developing countries. Natural Resource Issues No. 11. International Institute for Environment and Development, London.

Priscoli, J. and A. Wolf (2009) Managing and transforming water conflicts. Cambridge University Press.

Redford, K. and W. Adams (2009) Payment for ecosystem services and the challenge of saving nature. *Conservation Biology,* 23 (4) 785–7.

Rulli, M., A. Saviori and P. D'Odorica (2013) "Global land and water grabbing." *Proceedings of the National Academy of Sciences* 110(3): 892–97.

Saleth, R. M., and A. Dinar (2004) The Institutional Economics of Water: A Cross-Country Analysis of Institutions and Performance. Edward Elgar, Northampton, Mass., York: Cambridge University Press.

Schwartz, K. (2008) "The new public management: The future for reforms in the African water supply and sanitation sector?" *Utilities Policy* 16(1): 49–58.

Stanton, T., M. Echavarria, K. Hamilton and C. Ott (2010) State of Watershed Payments: An Emerging Marketplace. Ecosystem Marketplace. Available online: http://www.forest-trends.org/documents/files/doc_2438.pdf

Timmerman, J. (2015) Information needs for water management. Taylor & Francis Group.

Tsur, Y., T. Roe, R. Douklali and A. Dinar (2004) Pricing irrigation water: principles and cases from developing countries. Resources for the Future, UAS.

Woodhouse, P. and A. Ganho (2011). *Is water the hidden agenda of agricultural land acquisition in sub-Saharan Africa?* International Conference on Global Land Grabbing, Institute of Development Studies, 6–8 April. UK: University of Sussex.

Wunder, S. (2005) Payments for environmental services: some nuts and bolts. Occational Paper No. 42. Center for International Forestry Research, Indonesia.

Wunder, S. (2008) "Payments for environmental services and the poor: Concepts and preliminary evidence." *Environment and Development Economics* 13: 279–97.

WWAP (World Water Assessment Programme (2014) The United Nations World Water Development Report 2014: Water and Energy. Paris, UNESCO.

WWAP (World Water Assessment Programme) (2015) The United Nations World Water Development Report 2015: Water for a Sustainable World. Paris, UNESCO.

70 %

decrease in illegal water abstractions was recorded in the middle and lower sub-catchments between 2006–07, when the first water resources user associations were created in the Tana Catchment, and 2010.

2. Performance Assessment and Evaluation of Community Participation in Water Sector Governance

The case of Ngaciuma-Kinyaritha catchment, Mount Kenya Region

Joy A. Obando,[1] Cush N. Luwesi,[2] James M. Mathenge,[3] Wanja Kinuthia,[4] Philip P. Wambua,[5] Mary N. Mutiso,[6] Essam O. Bader[7]

Introduction

The Republic of Kenya initiated key reforms in 1999 in its water sector governance. These reforms culminated with the release of the Water Act 2002, which has been amended to comply with the devolved system enshrined in the Constitution of Kenya 2010. The Water Act 2002 instituted a separation between Water Service Providers (WSPs) and Water Resource Users' Associations (WRUA). In compliance with the new legislation, Ngaciuma-Kinyaritha stakeholders created a WRUA in that catchment in 2006, amid many Community Water Management Systems (CWMSs). The latter are not legally recognised for managing water resources or for supplying water services.

Should these CWMSs seek registration to qualify as WSPs? This is technically difficult for most "self-help" groups, and this study sought to assess the performance of the newly established key institutions among the CWMSs in Ngaciuma-Kinyaritha Catchment. To isolate the contribution of CWMSs to domestic water security a Performance Assessment and Evaluation (PAE) was conducted based on household survey data from 165 farmers and 36 in-depth interviews.

The findings reveal that Kenya can be credited with having succeeded in initiating and implementing a participatory water governance system, despite

---

1 Focal Region Manager, CGIAR Research Programme on Water, Land and Ecosystems (WLE) – Volta-Niger, IWMI-West Africa Office, CSIR Campus, PMB CT 112, Cantonments, Accra, Ghana

2. Corresponding Author: Dr Cush Ngonzo Luwesi. Email: C.Luwesi@cgiar.org
   Associate Professor, Department of Geography, Kenyatta University, PO Box 43844-00100, Nairobi, Kenya

3 Senior Research Scientist, Mount Kenya Research Programme, Kenya Wildlife Service, PO Box 22-10100, Nyeri, Kenya

4 Senior Researcher, Department of Zoology, National Museums of Kenya, PO Box 40658-00100, Nairobi, Kenya

5 Lecturer, Business Administration Department, Kenyatta University, PO Box 43844-00100, Nairobi, Kenya

6 Assistant Lecturer, Department of Community and Development Studies, South Eastern Kenya University, PO Box 170-90200, Kitui, Kenya

7 Associate Professor, Faculty of Agricultural Economics, Damietta University, PO Box 34517, New Damietta Egypt

various financial and investment challenges. Moreover, though not legally recognised, CWMSs have achieved almost a third of the targets of the water sector reforms in Ngaciuma-Kinyaritha Catchment, just like the registered WSPs and WRUAs. They need to be integrated into the new Water Act, which hopefully will be enacted in 2015. The latter has undergone a very long revision since 2012, owing to contention over the transfer of powers on water supply and water resources (Cap. 371 and 372) and other political interferences.

Purpose of the study

World water resources will be major casualties of global warming. Kundzewicz (2007) noted that, "There are three categories of water stress that would be exacerbated by climate change: (i) Too little; (ii) Too much; and (iii) Too dirty." Though Hulme et al. (2001) predicted increased precipitation in most Arid and Semi-Arid Lands (ASALs) of Kenya during dry periods, these and other humid areas will experience lower precipitation during almost the whole year. Therefore, visionary policies and legislation are needed to promote water security through local investment in water and land conservation (Huggins 2002). Community involvement in water resource management was the core objective of the water sector reforms initiated in Kenya in 1999. However, conservation of wetlands as a source of water and income generating activities there from emanating were not given prominence dispite Kenya being a signatory of the ramsar convention. These would have provided an incentive for sustainable local wetlands conservation and thus community water security (Macharia et al. 2010) To integrate local communities into such participatory water governance, the new Water Act (2002) instituted WRUAs in all the catchments amid many Water Service Providers (WSPs) by ignoring the traditional role of existing Community Water Management Systems (CWMSs) (Mathenge et al. 2014). Thenceforward, the Water Resource Management Authority (WRMA) could not integrate these CWMSs into its institutional framework in order to guide the development, supply, utilisation and conservation of water resources at the local level. Should these CWMSs therefore seek registration to qualify as WSPs? In legal terms the answer is a simple "yes," but registration is technically difficult for most "self-help" groups operating under customary law, which gave them all the mandates of the newly created WRUAs and WSPs. This study sought to uncover the implications of a ban on such traditional institutions on water security. A comparative assessment of the performance of CWMSs operating in Ngaciuma-Kinyaritha Catchment vis-à-vis the newly created WRUA and WSP was aimed at isolating their respective contributions to domestic water security in the Mount Kenya Region.

Literature review

Climate Impact on the Rural Economy of Kenya

Climatic water related hazards are predicted to escalate in regions where forests and wetlands have been depleted (Pachauri 2004; Ngonzo et al. 2010). The latter are known to absorb excess water during floods and soften the effects of droughts. Hence, the 2007/2008 Human Development Report (HDR) mentioned five interactive transmission mechanisms of climate impacts on the rural economy: (1) collapse of ecosystems; (2) increased coastal flooding and extreme weather events; (3) heightened water insecurity; (4) reduced agricultural productivity; and (5) increased health risks. The report concludes: "While the processes are already apparent in many countries, breaching the 2°C threshold would mark a qualitative shift: it would mark a transition to far greater ecological, social and economic damage" (UNDP 2007: P. 30).

An ecological disaster in the Kenyan rural economy may be explained in terms of extreme water deficiency or low soil moisture in farmlands, which lead to excessive water stress or desiccation of crops and plants, soil loss and mass movements, and massive loss of natural habitats (Brown 2001; UNEP 2009). The social disaster may be attributed to the effect of the El Niño Southern Oscillation (ENSO) associated with worsening vulnerability to drought and dry spells as well as other related extreme events (Downing 2003; Jaetzold et al. 2007). Finally, an economic disaster is generally associated with externalities emanating from environmental changes (Luwesi 2010). Consequently, legal and policy responses are key in achieving adaptation to and mitigation of water disasters in order to ensure water and food security in the course of climate change (Huggins 2002; Van Koppen 2007).

Legal and Policy Responses to Water Disasters in Kenya

Kenya has undergone several reforms to the governance of its water sector. Ngigi and Macharia (2007) report that from 1963 (independence) to 1997, the reforms targeted improvement of water quality and quantity through adequate financing mechanisms (GOK 1965). This was reiterated in the "Water for all by 2000" slogan in the 1974 National Water Master Plan (NWMP), which led to establishment of a national water development corporation in 1988 and a National Water Master Plan 2012 in 1992 (GOK 1999).

The first guidelines for community participation appeared in 1997, when the government invited the private sector to participate in a decentralised form of water governance (K'akumu 2008). These guidelines were formally released in 1999 as the National Policy on Water Resource Management and Development (GOK 1999). They were enacted as laws under the Water Act 2002 (GOK 2002) (Figure 1).

Figure 1: Legal framework of the Water Act 2002

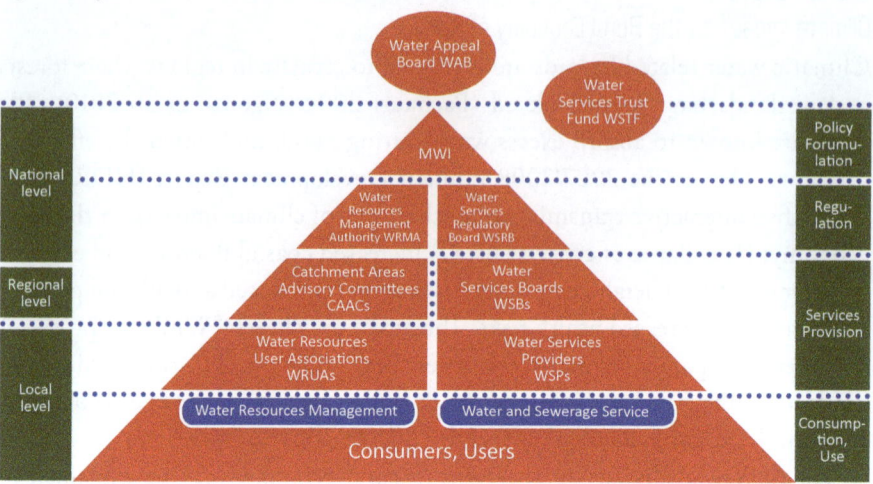

Source: GOK (2002)

Pursuant to the implementation of the Water Act 2002, the WRMA and Water Services Regulatory Board (WASREB) were established in 2005, followed by a National Water Resources Management Strategy (2007–09) and its integration into the 2007 Kenyan development blueprint, Kenya Vision 2030. In 2012, a new bill was introduced into parliament to align the provisions of the Water Act 2002 with the devolution enshrined in the Constitution of Kenya 2010 (GOK 2010; 2014). This gave rise to the development of the National Water Master Plan 2030 (JICA and GoK 2013).

Community Involvement in Water Resources Management
The global community recognises the right of both men and women to participate in development projects. In fact, the Rio Declaration on Environment and Development (UNSD 1992) stated: "environmental issues are best handled with the participation of all concerned citizens, at the relevant level …" (Principle 10). One of the four principles put forward at the Dublin Water Conference in 1992 was that "Water development and management should be based upon a participatory approach …" (Förch et al. 2005). These principles have long been stressed and widely accepted by international, national and local levels of government, even if they have not been implemented by all governments (Crow and Sultana 2002).

Nishimoto (2003) reports that a World Bank review strongly encouraged women's participation in 121 rural water supply projects, which were found to be effective and sustainable. Maharaj et al. (1999) reveals that a government programme in Malawi was at risk of collapse when male-dominated committees were collecting fees. A change of regulations that assigned 60 per cent women and 40 per cent men to committees led to improved management of the programme. Similarly, the success of the Philippines Communal Irrigation Project was attributed to the integration of women into project operations (Nishimoto 2003). As in Malawi, the involvement of women increased payment of fees, as women controlled household finances.

Hence, in the "World Water Vision" Cosgrove and Rijsberman (2000) cite public participation in the management and conservation of water resources as a "real revolution." But, this will only come true if all stakeholders are empowered to manage their own resources. Yet, community participation in the implementation of the Kenyan Water Act 2002 does not include communal "Self-Help Groups," which are acknowledged as managing the catchment area while providing water services to all (Mathenge et al. 2013). Instead, the law delegates water catchment conservation to the WRUAs registered by WRMA, while the provision of water, sanitation and sewage services is the sole responsibility of WSPs legally licensed by the WASREB (Were et al. 2006).

The CWMSs existing where such legal institutions do not operate are therefore challenged in discharging their communal mandate of guiding the development, supply, utilisation and conservation of local water resources. Should these CWMSs seek registration to qualify as WSPs and/or WRUAs? This study will shed light on their contribution to water security under changing legal environments in Ngaciuma-Kinyaritha.

Methodology
Geographical Setting of the Study Area

Ngaciuma-Kinyaritha is a sub-catchment of the Tana River emanating from Mount Kenya. It covers an area of 167 km^2, with an estimated population of about 65,000 and a density of 390 persons/km^2 (KNBS 2010). The catchment is bound by longitudes 37.5° E and 37.75° E, and latitudes 0.04° N and 0.15° N (Figure 2).

The catchment spans three coffee agro-ecological zones (AEZ), namely Upper Midland AEZ 1 (UM 1), the coffee-tea zone; Upper Midland AEZ 2 (UM 2), the main coffee zone; and Upper Midland AEZ 3 (UM 3), the marginal coffee zone (Jaetzold et al. 2007). Most of the soils are basaltic volcanic rock, except in the forested parts, with altitudes ranging from 1,120 m to 2,600 m. They are geologically young soils, thus poorly consolidated and susceptible to erosion and mass movement, as well as to high infiltration and seepage rates, especially on hillslopes (Förch et al. 2008). This justifies the presence of CWMSs to manage the little surface drainage at source, including Lake Nkunga crater, with its three springs and a sub-surface outlet joining Ngaciuma and Kinyaritha streams.

Figure 2: Map of Ngaciuma-Kinyaritha Catchment

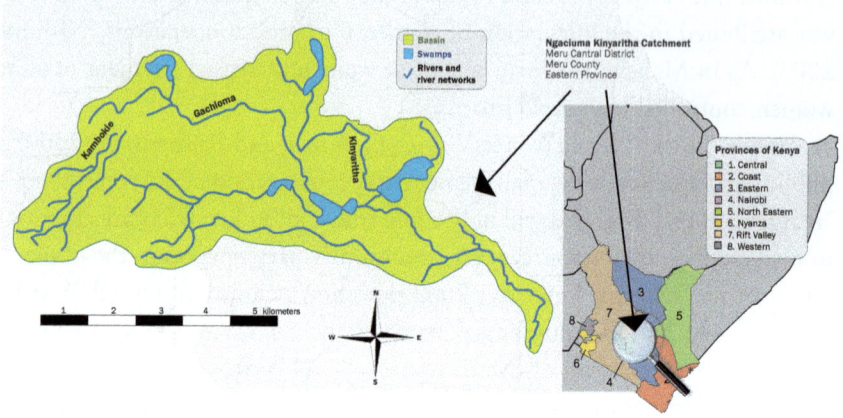

Source: Alufa (2010)

Sampling Strategy and Sample Size

Ngaciuma-kinyaritha Catchment was purposely selected because it was one of the pilot catchments designated by WRMA for WRUA formation in 2006. A stratified random sampling was used to divide the catchment into three different hydro-ecological zones, Ngaciuma, Kinyaritha Minor and Kinyaritha Major. In total, 177 households were randomly selected at 5 % significance level, 5 % estimate precision and 10 % true population proportion. These were affiliates of 32 CWMSs and 1 WRUA.

Data Collection

Data used in this study mainly encompass socioeconomic information collected during a household survey (using questionnaires), in-depth interviews (involving 36 local administration officers) and a Focus Group Discussion (FGD) with eight key informants from the 32 CWMSs. A documentary review made possible the gathering of secondary data on water resources and demand within the six basins of Kenya and the three major nodes of the Ngaciuma-Kinyaritha River.

Data Analysis and Interpretation of Results

Data collected were inputted, pre-processed and analysed using SPSS and MS Excel spreadsheets. The results relating to the performance of WRMA and WASREB were retrieved from official government and private documents. However, the socioeconomic factors emphasised during the survey, interviews and FGD were subjected to a robust Performance Assessment and Evaluation (PAE) involving both qualitative and quantitative techniques along with a triangulation of data and methods (Furubo 2009).

The only qualitative technique used in the robust PAE involved pattern or content analysis. The remaining part of the analysis used quantitative techniques supported by a scorecard of key actors involved in the study, namely a WSP (MEWASS), a WRUA (NGAKINYA WRUA) and 32 anonymous CWMSs. Utility ratios on the efficiency and effectiveness of each of the above institutions were derived by comparing descriptive statistics with the targets of the NGAKINYA WRUA SCMP 2007–2010 (Rogers 2005; Kazbekov et al. 2009). These results were presented in tables and in a web chart to shed light on the contribution of local CWMSs to ensuring domestic water security among the WRUAs and WSPs operating in the Ngaciuma-Kinyaritha Catchment.

Results and discussion
Overall Performance of the 2002 Water Sector Reforms

Water Resources Management: The Government of Kenya (GoK) through WRMA may be credited with reaching a landmark in its water resource management targets. WRMA (2010) reports that GoK established six WRMA regional offices in 2005 in order to tackle inappropriate farming practices leading to land degradation, water crises and resource conflicts among upstream and downstream users. These encompassed: (a) Lake Victoria North Catchment Area (LVNCA), covering 18,374 km^2; (b) Lake Victoria South Catchment Area (LVSCA): 31,734 km^2; (c) Rift Valley Catchment Area (RVCA): 130,452 km^2; (d) Athi Catchment Area (ACA): 58,639 km^2; (e) Tana Catchment Area (TCA): 126,026 km^2; and, (f) Ewaso Ng'iro North Catchment Area (ENNCA), covering 210,226 km^2.

Besides the operationalisation of WRMA, Catchment Areas Advisory Committees (CAACs) were also put in place to advise WRMA in accomplishing its mandate. This led to the creation of the first WRUAs in the Tana Catchment (Bwathonaro and Ngaciuma-kinyaritha sub-catchments) in 2006–07. Also, the first Sub-Catchment Management Plans (SCMPs) were developed in each pilot catchment area during the same period. By 2009, each of the six WRMA regional offices had developed its Catchment Management Strategy (CMS), and over US$ 1,800,000 (KES 126,104,300) had been collected from water users. This development was explained by the increased number of WRUAs across the country to about 292 in 2010, 80 being mature and having SCMPs. Besides, a reduction by over 30 % of illegal water abstractions was recorded in the upper sub-catchments, while in the middle and lower sub-catchments a more than 70 % decrease was recorded. Finally, about 21.9 % of large water users and 78.1 % of small users were complying with water rules and regularly paying their water fees. Only seven prosecutions were initiated by the Water Appeal Boards (WABs) and parties complied with the decisions.

However, new developments are afoot in the Kenyan water sector ahead of

Table 1: Projected water balance in Kenya (millions of m³)

Catchment Area	2010			2030			2050		
	Water Resources (a)	Water Demand (b)	(b)(a)	Water Resources (c)	Water Demand (d)	(d)(c)	Water Resources (e)	Water Demand (f)	(f)(e)
LVNCA	4,742	228	5 %	5,077	1,337	26 %	5,595	1,573	28 %
LVSCA	4,975	385	8 %	5,937	2,953	50 %	7,195	3,251	45 %
RVCA	2,559	357	14 %	3,147	1,494	47 %	3,903	1,689	43 %
ACA	1,503	1,145	76 %	1,634	4,586	281 %	2,043	5,202	255 %
TCA	6,533	891	14 %	7,828	8,241	105 %	7,891	8,476	107 %
ENNCA	2,251	212	9 %	3,011	2,857	95 %	1,810	2,950	163 %
Total	22,564	3,218	14 %	26,634	21,468	81 %	28,437	23,141	81 %

Sources: JICA and GoK (2013)

the implementation of the devolution enshrined in the Constitution of Kenya 2010. The proposed Water Act 2014 suggests that WRMA will be upgraded to the status of Water Resources Regulatory Agency at the national level, and "Basin Water Regulatory Boards" at the basin level (under section 9); and CAACs will become "Basin Water Resources Committees" (under section 23) (GOK 2014). The new legislation has also proposed the creation of "new agencies, such as 'Water Works Development Board' and 'National Water Harvesting and Storage Authority'" (WaterCap 2014).

In line with the constitution, the national government will have to conserve catchment areas, develop water service infrastructures and monitor water service quality. Local governments will have to implement national policies at the county level to supplement infrastructure development for resource exploitation (GOK 2014). However, there are still gaps with regard to: (1) the capacity of institutions to manage water, sewage and drainage services as well as wastewater reclamation and disaster management at county level; and (2) the separation of regulation and implementation functions among the new bodies. These challenges need to be addressed as fast as possible to mitigate the deficits in water resources projected by 2030 in ACA, TCA and ENNCA (Table 1). Nonetheless, increased water resources and demand are foreseen in each basin, but with a reverse trend for water resources in 2050 in the ASALs, especially in ENNCA. Higher water demands of more than 40 % are predicted over water resources in ACA and Ewaso Ng'iro North Catchment Area. This will be driven by demand for irrigation water as proposed by the Kenya Vision 2030 (Table 2).

Water Services Provision: According to the Kenya national census of 2009, only 14 % of households in rural areas reported having access to tap water, while a majority fetched water from springs, wells and boreholes (42 %), streams (31 %) and dams and ponds (6 %) (Figure 3).

Table 2: Projected water demand by sub-sector (millions of m³)

Subsector	Year 2010 (a)	Year 2030 (b)	(b)(a) (%)	Year 2050 (c)	(c)(a) (%)
Domestic	1,186	2,561	216	3,657	308
Industrial	125	280	224	613	490
Irrigation	1,602	18,048	1,127	18,048	1,127
Livestock	255	497	195	710	278
Wildlife	8	8	100	8	100
Fisheries	42	74	176	105	250
Total	3,218	21,468	667	23,141	719

Sources: JICA and GoK (2013)

Figure 3: Water service accessibility in rural area

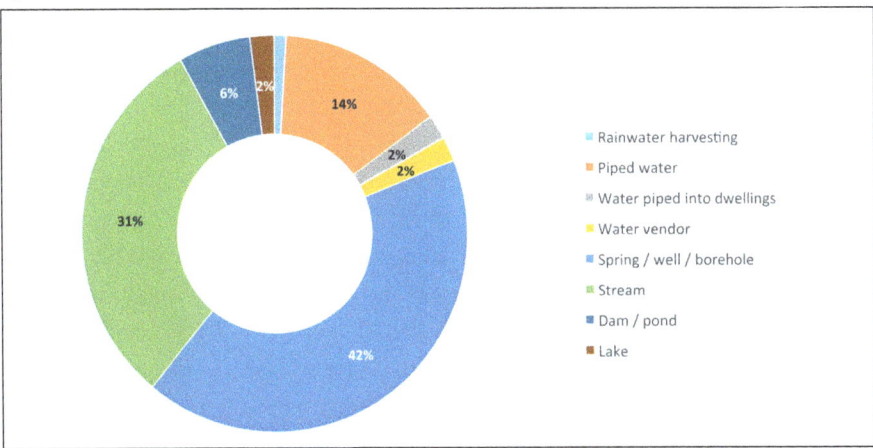

Source: KNBS 2010

However, 38 % accessed tap water in urban settings, and 14 % even had water connections to their homes. Only 24 % had to use springs, wells and boreholes, 13 % water vendors and 8 % streams (Figure 4).

This situation called for the creation of Water Services Regulatory Board to license Water Services' Boards (WSBs). The latter have the mandate of developing water infrastructure in each region served by WASREB, and award permits to WSPs in major cities and to rural areas under WSB control. Strategic actions adopted by WASREB for financing water infrastructure included: (i) tariffs, fees and fines to cover transaction costs for Operations and Maintenance (O&M); (ii) governmental Medium Term Expenditure Framework (MTEF) to collect taxes from domestic taxpayers to finance water infrastructure development; and (iii) donors and International Financial Institutions (IFIs) leverage to fund additional investments in water infrastructure (Luwesi 2011; WASREB and WSP 2011).

Performance of the Water Sector in Kenya: The performance report by WASREB (2012) shows some improvement in the performance of 46 WSPs in 2010-2011 compared to the year 2008 (Table 3).

Figure 4: Water services in urban settings

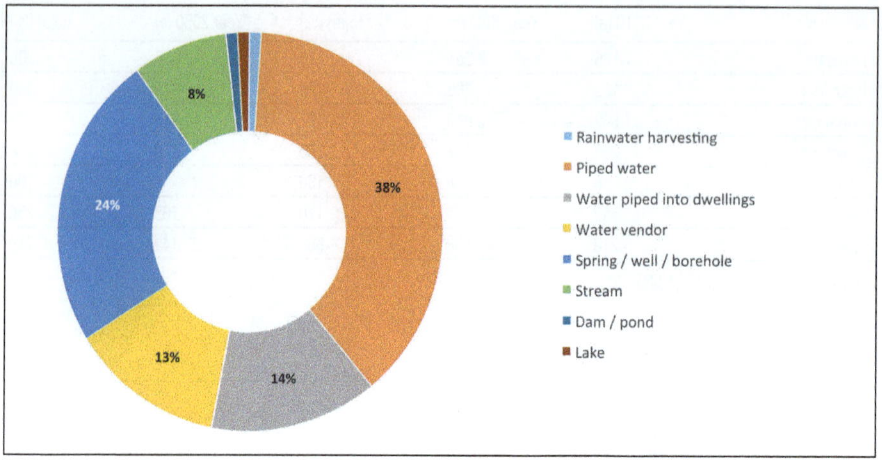

- Rainwater harvesting
- Piped water: 38%
- Water piped into dwellings
- Water vendor: 13%
- Spring / well / borehole: 14%
- Stream: 24%
- Dam / pond
- Lake: 8%

Source: KNBS (2010)

The most performing WSPs were classified into three types: (Type 1) those not having achieved the full cost of O&M; (Type 2) those having covered full O&Ms but unable to repay pending debts; and (Type 3) those having covered between 100 % and 150 % of O&M costs and partly or fully repaid their debts. Most WSPs lacked consistency, except for 21 Type 3 cases located in major towns such as Nairobi, Mombasa, Kisumu, Nyeri and Meru. Hence, WASREB and WSP (2011) could stress on the more urgent financing needs for sanitation infrastructure, even in urban areas where households were connected to water and sewerage lines. Moreover, water sector financing in Kenya, especially infrastructure development, becomes a burden for IFIs and donors since they carry a 56.5 % share of the total budget (WASREB 2012). These financial challenges may hamper the smooth implementation of water sector reforms.

Without proper tariffs, the Kenyan water sector will depend heavily on donor and IFI funding for infrastructure development. Yet, the current international financial environment is not such as to enable the Kenyan government

Table 3: WSP performance in 2010–2011

Indicators	2008/2009	2008/2010
Number WSPs	46	39 %
Number WSPs with sewerage systems	21	23
Water Coverage	46 %	67%
Sanitation Coverage	47 %	67 %
Sewerage coverage (Nairobi)	30 %	28 %
Sewerage coverage (Mombasa)	7 %	4 %
Average sewerage coverage (Kenya)	15 %	15 %

Source: WASREB (2012)

to raise sufficient funds by 2015 to achieve its strategic targets for water, sewage and drainage s infrastructure, notably 40 % to 70% for water supply and 5 % to 10 % for sewage and drainage services in rural areas, and 60 % to 80 % for water supply and 30 % to 40 % for sewage and drainage services in urban areas (Bouwer 2003; AMCW et al. 2006; GOK 2008; World Bank et al. 2008).

Besides, the prospects of a water balance in Kenya by 2050 are gloomy in all the major basins. It is clear that irrigation demands associated with the targets in the Kenya Vision 2030 are unrealistic and need to be reduced (Falkenmark and Rockström 2004; Mogaka et al. 2006; Mumma et al. 2011). Therefore, water sector sustainability may be achieved through inclusive financing and management of water resources and related infrastructures by communities (Dyszynski 2010). The following section examines the contribution of CWMSs in ensuring water security in the Ngaciuma-Kinyaritha Catchment.

CWMSs' Contribution to Domestic Water Security in Ngaciuma-Kinyaritha

Performance Assessment and Evaluation: CWMS performance in managing water resources and providing water services in Ngaciuma-Kinyaritha recorded a total ratio of 53.6 %, while their WRUA and WSP counterparts fared "fairly well" (62.2 % and 54.4 %, respectively). Even so, their shared contribution to water security was as "fairly poor," that is below 40 % and above 30 % (Table 4). In effect, CWMSs' contribution to water supply sustainability and environmental management was rated "fairly poor" (below 50 %), owing to insufficient and inadequate technological means and the lack of contingent plans to address water disasters (Table 5).

Nonetheless, all water institutions performed "fairly well" in water resource management and social inclusion with overall ratios rising above 60 % (Table 6). CWMSs were particularly lauded for being socially inclusive, especially when it came to decision-making and conflict resolution (60 %) and to inte-

Table 4: Performance utility ratios of water institutions in Ngaciuma-Kinyaritha

CONTRIBUTION	CWMS		MEWASS		NGAKINYA WRUA	
	Rate	Performance	Rate	Performance	Rate	Performance
Water supply sustainability and environmental management	50.0 %	Fairly well	54.4 %	Fairly well	62.2 %	Fairly poor
Water resource management and social inclusion	62.2 %	Fairly well	60.0 %	Fairly well	71.1 %	Fairly well
Economic development and business success	36.0 %	Fairly well	68.0 %	Fairly well	68.0 %	Fairly poor
Farming water development and profitability	62.0 %	Fairly well	46.0 %	Fairly poor	62.0 %	Fairly well
Rating	53.6 %	Fairly well	57.1 %	Fairly well	66.1 %	Fairly well
Performance	30.3 %	Fairly Poor	32.3 %	Fairly Poor	37.4 %	Fairly Poor

Source: Mathenge et al. (2014)

Table 5: Water services provision and sustainability in Ngaciuma-Kinyaritha

No	CONTRIBUTION	CWMS	MEWASS	NGAKINYA WRUA
1.	Reduced distance to water source	50	80	60
2.	Increased water quality	40	70	40
3.	Enhanced water services affordability	80	50	70
4.	Water supply self-sufficiency	30	80	60
5.	Catchment management capability	80	30	90
6.	Drought prevention /preparedness	30	0	40
7.	Water management/ services modernisation	40	80	60
8.	Soil conservation effectiveness	60	20	80
9.	Water conservation effectiveness	40	80	60
	Rating	50 %	54.4 %	62.2 %
	Performance	Fairly Poor	Fairly Well	Fairly Well

Source: Mathenge et al. (2014)

Table 6: Water resource management and social inclusion in Ngaciuma-Kinyaritha

No	CONTRIBUTION	CWMS	MEWASS	NGAKINYA WRUA
1.	Local culture on water supply/ management	100	75	80
2.	Gender sensitive water supply / management (women and men equality)	100	75	100
3.	Welfare improvement	50	50	60
4.	Decreased frequency of drought	50	0	60
5.	Reduced distance for fetching water	50	90	60
6.	Reduced time for fetching water	50	80	60
7.	Reduced cases of water borne diseases	40	80	60
8.	Public consultation/ involvement in decision-making	60	20	80
9.	Decreased cases of conflict on water use	60	70	80
	Rating	62.2 %	60 %	71.1 %
	Performance	Fairly Well	Fairly Well	Fairly Well

Source: Mathenge et al. (2014)

grating local culture and gender sensitivity in their daily management (100 %) (Table 6). However, technological inefficiency was a hindrance to improving community welfare through notably good water hygiene practices and drought control measures, as well in as in reducing the time and distance for fetching water (50 %). Thus, they were rated "fairly well" (62.2 %).

CWMSs' contribution to economic development and business success was found to be fairly ineffective (50 %), and thus could not add value to the existing infrastructure in the catchment (25 %). They could not control water price fluctuations due to seasonality (50 %) or foster new businesses (35 %).

Table 7: Economic development and business success in Ngaciuma-Kinyaritha

No	CONTRIBUTION	CWMS	MEWASS	NGAKINYA WRUA
1.	Water supply/ management network coverage	20	60	90
2.	Use of water charges (tariff/ price)	50	100	100
3.	New investments in irrigation schemes in the area	25	20	35
4.	Increased economic activities due to water development	35	75	40
5.	Reduced seasonal variability of water cost	50	85	75
	Rating	36 %	68 %	68 %
	Performance	Fairly Poor	Fairly Good	Fairly Good

Source: Mathenge et al. (2014)

Table 8: Water development and farming profitability in Ngaciuma-Kinyaritha

No	CONTRIBUTION	CWMS	MEWASS	NGAKINYA WRUA
1.	Water conservation and rain harvesting for agriculture	60	20	60
2.	Reduced water cost in farming	50	30	40
3.	Increased yield in farming	40	60	50
4.	Farmers adhering to community water management system	100	20	80
5.	Farmers paying for more effective and efficient water management	60	100	80
	Rating	62 %	46 %	62 %
	Performance	Fairly well	Fairly Poor	Fairly well

Source: Mathenge et al. (2014)

Hence, their overall performance in the economic and business sector was recorded as "fairly poor" ratio (36 %) (Table 7).

Table 8 reveals that CWMSs like NGAKINYA WRUA have a fair capability (62 %) in developing water resources to ensure farming profitability, which WSPs do not have. CWMSs have a strong influence on community beliefs and motivations and can play a key role in mobilising community members, especially women, to participate in the implementation of water and soil conservation measures in the catchment. In addition, they can encourage farmers to harvest rainwater and pay for environmental services, even though they have limited capability to manage water costs and increase farm yield. Hence, globally rated, CWMSs' water governance capability in Ngaciuma-Kinyaritha Catchment was rated as "fairly well," but their share in achieving water security was "fairly poor," just like other water institutions (Figure 5).

Discussion on CWMSs' Contribution to Domestic Water Security

With the ongoing implementation of water sector reforms, WSPs (notably MEWASS) and the NGAKINYA WRUA are wholly able to achieve nearly 70 % of water security targets in Ngaciuma-Kinyaritha Catchment. The remaining one-third can be attributed to the CWMSs, mostly known as "Self-Help" groups.

Figure 5: Overall performance of CWMSs in Ngaciuma-Kinyaritha

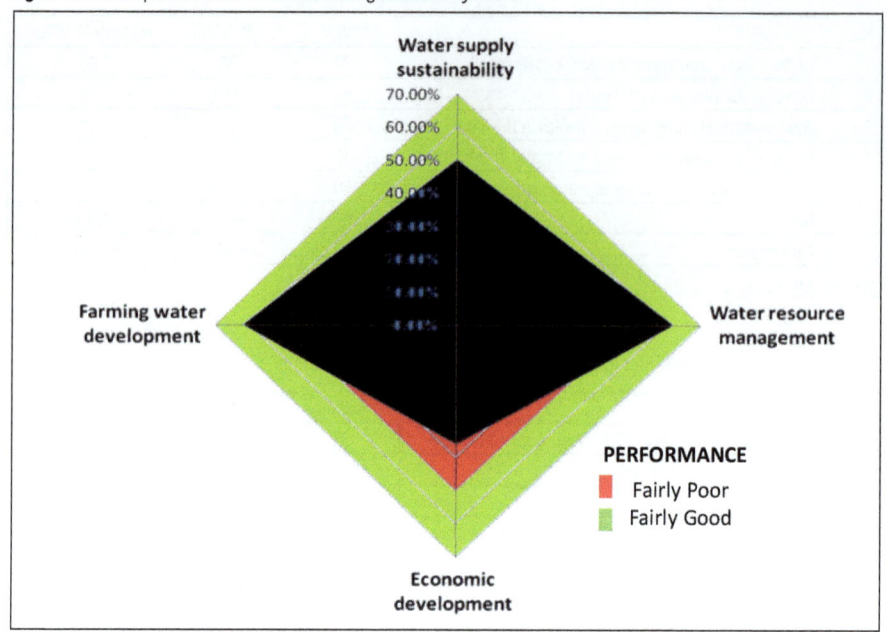

Note: The black polygon in the centre represents CWMS performance in Ngaciuma-Kinyaritha

This disparity in the management and usage of water has resulted in poor performance of water projects in Kenya and other developing countries (Maharaj et al. 1999; Suda 2000).

Therefore, the future welfare of community living in Ngaciuma-Kinyaritha Catchment will depend on cooperation among all established institutions both at local and national levels. Policy-makers, on one hand, and local community leaders, on the other, need to define a coherent management framework and enforcement mechanisms (Ayling and Kelly 1997). When government policies and laws start conflicting with local people's traditions and cultural practices, one can expect progressive degradation of the quality and quantity of water flowing in the catchment (Shivoga et al. 2007). This is typical of the current legal environment for the water sector in Kenya, where CWMSs are significantly excluded from both catchment management and rural water supply. Negative environmental impacts are foreseen in areas where no WRUA is operational if CWMSs collapse or decide to give up ahead of the enforcement of the Water Act 2014 (Lelo et al. 2005).

Conclusion and recommendations

The status of water security in Kenya in general and in Ngaciuma-Kinyaritha Catchment in particular, is volatile and needs to be urgently addressed. There is thus a need for a more inclusive and multi-pronged approach to solving the many problems facing catchment areas in the country. Sustainability in water resources and sanitation services also requires adequate investment in infrastructure development. When coupled with good infrastructure and technological innovativeness, community participation in the development of water and sanitation infrastructures may achieve the targets of the water sector reforms under the stewardship of CWMSs. Though informal, these self-help groups are already achieving 30 % of the targets of the reforms in Ngaciuma-Kinyaritha Catchment, just like any WSP or WRUA. Hence, there is a need for large-scale inclusion of the masses through dialogue forums surrounding water legislation to foster community participation and ease the water inequalities facing certain stakeholders. The latter should be empowered politically, legally and financially to meet their demands for water in the course of climate change.

Key policies and research implications

The water crisis is the result of the current legal environment in Kenya, which technically locks traditional CWMSs out of the water business to the benefit of WRUAs and WSPs. CWMSs are significantly excluded from both catchment management and rural water supply. Yet, in areas where no WRUAs and WSPs are operational, water security is crucial, owing to negative environmental impacts, lack of water infrastructure and/or the collapse of CWMSs. This collapse is foreseeable where CWMSs are banned or forced to give up ahead of the enforcement of the revised Water Act 2014. Hence, it is imperative for the Government of Kenya to include all stakeholders in the ongoing dialogue surrounding the new act. These discussions shall also consider recommendations from The *Ramsar Convention*, formally known as the *Convention on Wetlands of International Importance*, which advocates for the conservation and sustainable utilization of wetlands, especially waterfowl habitats. By recognizing the fundamental ecological functions of wetlands and their economic, cultural, scientific, and recreational value, the new water act would empower CWMSs to enforce laws that mitigate adverse environmental impacts going on in the catchment.

Moreover, water security also involves the sustainability of water resources and services. This requires adequate investment in infrastructure development and technological innovation. The government and its institutional partners must therefore ensure cost-recovery through tariffs and taxes to provide for water investments and minimise dependence on donor funding. Community participation in financing the development of water and sanitation infrastructure thus becomes very significant in achieving the targets of the water sector reforms. Researchers are particularly urged to identify innovative economic tactics to raise funding for agricultural water development through mechanisms such as Payment for Watershed Services (PWS) and blended financial instruments. There is also a need for assessing alternative technological and environmental measures implementable at small catchment level by CWMSs to ensure Green Water Saving (GWS) in wider basins in the country, namely Athi, Ewaso-N'giro, Lake Victoria North, Lake Victoria South, Rift Valley and Tana. Enhancement of the capability of CWMS managers in strategic water business planning and technological innovation may be achieved through implementation of new professional curricula at the Kenya Water Institute (KEWI).

References

Alufa, S. (2010) Adoption of Soil and Water Conservation Technologies for Sustainable Watershed Management and Planning in Ngaciuma Sub-Catchment, Kenya. MSc Thesis (Unpublished). Nairobi: Kenyatta University

AMCEN-African Ministerial Conference on Environment, UNEP-United Nations Environment Program and CLIMATE ANALYTICS (2013) "Climate-change Impacts, Adaptation Challenges and Costs for Africa." Africa's Adaptation Gap Technical Report. Nairobi: UNEP, Regional Office for Africa (ROA).

AMCW-African Ministers' Council on Water, AfDB-African Development Bank, EUWI- EU Water Initiative, WSP-Water sanitation Program and UNDP-United Nations Development Program (2006) Getting Africa on Track to Meet the MDGs on Water Supply and Sanitation – A Status Overview of Sixteen African Countries. Nairobi: AMCW.

Ayling, R. and K. Kelly. (1997) "Dealing with conflict: Natural resources and dispute resolution." *Commonwealth Forestry Review* 76 (3): 182–85.

Bouwer, H. (2003) "Integrated Water management for the 21st Century: Problems and Solutions." *Food Agriculture and Environment* 1 (1): 18–127.

Brown, L.R. (2001) *Eco-Economy: Building an economy for the Earth*. New York: Norton.

Cosgrove, W.J. and F.R. Rijsberman (2000) *World Water Vision: Making Water Everybody's Business*. Earthscan: London.

Crow, B. and F. Sultana (2002) "Gender, class, and access to water: Three cases in a poor and crowed delta." *Society and Natural Resources* 15: 709–24.

Downing, T. (2003) "Linking sustainable livelihoods and global climate change in vulnerable food systems." *Die Erde* 133: 363–78.

Dyszynski, J. (2010) UNEP AdaptCost: Economics of climate change adaptation in Africa's water sector. Oxford: Stockholm Environment Institute.

Falkenmark, M. and J. Rockström (2004) *Balancing Water for Humans and Nature*. London: Earthscan.

Förch, G., R. Winnegge and S. Thiemann (eds) (2005) DAAD Alumni Summer School 2005: Topics of Integrated Water Resources Management. Weiterbilding in Siegen 18.

Förch, G., R. Winnegge and S. Thiemann (eds.) (2008) DAAD Alumni Summer School: Water Demand in Participatory Watershed Management – Ngaciuma-Kinyaritha Watershed, Kenya, Final Report (November). Meru: Universitat Siegen and Kenyatta University.

Furubo, J-E. (2009) Evaluation and Performance Audit: Rationale, questions and Methods. Speech at the Cours des Comptes (France) Conference. URL: www.riksrevionen.se. Accessed on 03. 07. 2009.

GOK- Government of Kenya (1965) The Agriculture Act, CAP 318. An act of parliament to promote and maintain a stable agriculture. Nairobi: Government Printer.

GOK- Government of Kenya (1999) National Policy on Water Resources Management and Development, Sessional Paper No. 1 of 1999. Nairobi: Government Printer.

GOK- Government of Kenya (2002) The Water Act, 2002. Kenya Gazette Supplement No. 107 (Acts No. 9). Nairobi: Government Printer, pp 287–413.

GOK- Government of Kenya (2008) Public expenditure Review, 2008 Nairobi: Government Printer. Available at http://www.planning.go.ke/ Government of Kenya.

GOK- Government of Kenya (2010) The Constitution of Kenya, 2010. Kenya Law Reports, Laws of Kenya. Nairobi: National Council for Law Reporting.

GOK- Government of Kenya (2014) The Water Bill, 2014 (Draft Bill introduced into parliament for approval). Available: http://kenyalaw.org/kl/fileadmin/pdfdownloads/bills/2014/WaterBill2014.pdf

Huggins, C. (2002) "Water policy and law in a water-scarce country: Implications for Smallholder Irrigation in Kenya." In: H.G. Blank, C.M. Mutero and H. Murray-Rust (eds) *The Changing Face of Irrigation in Kenya*. Colombo: International Water Management Institute, pp 277–300.

Hulme, M., R. Doherty, T. Ngara, T., M. New and D. Lister (2001) "African Climate Change: 1900-2100." *Climate Research* 17: 145–68.

Jaetzold, R., H. Schmidt, B. Hortnetz and C. Shisanya (2007) "Natural conditions and farm management information – Part C East Kenya, Subpart C1 Eastern Province." In: Ministry of Agriculture and German Technical Cooperation (GTZ) *Farm Management Handbooks of Kenya*, Vol. II. Nairobi, pp. 1–571.

JICA- Japanese International Cooperation Agency and GOK- Government of Kenya (2013) The Development of the National Water Master Plan 2030 (Final Draft). Nairobi: Nippon Koei.

K'akumu, O.A. (2008) "Mainstreaming the participatory approach in water resource governance: The 2002 water law in Kenya." *Development* 51: 56–62.

Kazbekov, J., I. Abdullaev, H. Manthrithilake, A. Qureshi and K. Jumaboev (2009) "Evaluating planning and delivery performance of water user associations (WUA) in Osh Province, Kyrgyzstan." *Agricultural Water Management* 96: 1259–67.

KNBS- Kenya National Bureau of Statistics (2010) Kenya 2009 Population and Housing Census. Government Printer, Nairobi.

Lelo, F., W. Chiuri and M. Jenkins (2005) "Managing the River Njoro Watershed, Kenya: Conflicting laws, policies, and community priorities." In: Republic of South Africa (ed.), *African Water Laws: Plural Legislative Frameworks for Rural Water Management in Africa*. Johannesburg.

Luwesi, C. (2010) Hydro-economic Inventory in a Changing Environment: An assessment of the efficiency of farming water demand under fluctuating rainfall regimes in semi-arid lands of South-East Kenya. Saarbrücken: Lambert Academic.

Luwesi, C.N. (ed) (2011) "Innovative Ways in Financing the Water Sector." SWAP/ bfz Workshop Report, 7–11 November. Mombasa: BFZ – Bavarian Finance Center and WaterCap

Macharia, J. M., Thenya T. and G. G. Nderitu (2010) "Management of Highland Wetlands in Central Kenya: The Importance of Community Education, Awareness and Ecotourism in Biodiversity Conservation. Biodiversity: Journal of Life on Earth. 11 (1 & 2) 85–90

Maharaj, N., A. Kusum, M. Garcia Vargas and G. Richardson (1999) Mainstreaming Gender in Water Resources Management: Why and How. Background Paper for the World Water Vision 1999. Paris: World Water Council.

Mathenge, J., C. Ngonzo, C. Shisanya, I. Mahiri, R. Akombo and M. Mutiso (2014) "Community Participation in Water Sector Governance in Kenya: A Performance Based Appraisal of Community Water Management Systems in Ngaciuma-Kinyaritha Catchment, Tana Basin, Mount Kenya Region." *International Journal of Innovative Research and Development* 3(5): 783–92.

Mogaka, H., S. Gichere, R. Davis and R. Hirji (eds)(2006) Climate Variability and Water Resources Degradation in Kenya. Improving Water Resources Development and Management. World Bank Working Paper No. 69.

Mumma, A., M. Lane, E. Kairu, A. Tuinhof and R. Hirji (2011) *Kenya groundwater governance case study. Water papers* (June). Washington: World Bank, Water and Sanitation Program (WSP).

Ngigi, A. and D. Macharia (2007) *Kenya Water Sector Overview*. Nairobi: IT Power East Africa.

Ngonzo, C., C. Shisanya and J. Obando (2010) "Land use and water demand under a changing climate: Experiences of smallholder farmers from Muooni." In S.P. Saikia (ed) *Climate Change*. Assam: International Book Distributors, pp. 117–40.

Nishimoto, S. (2003) *Mainstreaming Gender in Water Management: A Practical Journey to Sustainability. A Resource Guide*. New York: Environmentally Sustainable Development Group, UNDP/ Bureau for Development Policy.

Rogers, J. (2005) "A standardized performance assessment and evaluation model for community water systems." PhD thesis, University of Virginia.

Shivoga, W., M. Muchiri, S. Kibichi, J. Odanga, S. Miller, T. Baldyga, E. Enanga and M. Gichaba (2007) "Influences of land use/cover on water quality in the upper and middle reaches of River Njoro, Kenya." *Lakes and Reservoirs Research and Management* 12: 97–105.

Suda, C. (2000) "Gender, culture and environmental conservation in Western Kenya: Contextualizing community participation and the choice of techniques." *Nordic Journal of African Studies* 9(1): 31–48.

UNDP- United Nations Development Program (2007) Human Development Report 2007/ 2008 – Fighting Climate Change – Human Solidarity in a Divided World. New York: UNDP. Available at: http://hdr.undp.org/sites/default/files/reports/268/hdr_20072008_en_complete.pdf

UNEP- United Nations Environment Program (2009) Kenya: Atlas of Our Changing Environment. Nairobi: UNEP, Division of Early Warning and Assessment (DEWA).

UNSD- United Nations Sustainable Development (1992) Agenda 21. United Nations Conference on Environment and Development Rio de Janeiro, Brazil, 3–14 June. Available at: http://sustainabledevelopment.un.org/content/documents/Agenda21.pdf.

Van Koppen, B. (ed.)(2007) Community-Based Water Law and Water Resource Management Reform in Developing Countries. London: CABI.

WASREB and WSP (2011) Financing Urban Water Services in Kenya – Utility Shadow Credit Ratings. Nairobi: Water Services Regulatory Board (WASREB).

WASREB (2012) "A performance review of Kenya's water services sector, 2010/11." *Impact*, Issue No. 5.

WaterCap (2014) Water bill dialogue. WaterCap Newsletter (May).

Were, E., B. Swallow and J. Roy (2006) Water, women and local social organization in the Western Kenya highlands. ICRAF Working Paper no. 12. Nairobi. World Agroforestry Centre, CAPRI Working Paper #51. Available at: www.capri.cgiar.org

54 %

of the farmers and key informants rated the Kauti Irrigation Water Users' Association's overall contribution to social welfare and economic development as *fair*, in the evaluation of the green water saving schemes implemented in the Muooni Catchment in Kenya.

3. Climate Change, Pro-Poor Schemes and Water Inequality

Strengths and Weaknesses of Kauti Irrigation Water Users' Association, Kenya

Cush Ngonzo Luwesi,[1] Wanja Kinuthia,[2] Mary N. Mutiso,[3] Rose A. Akombo,[4] Dzigbodi A. Doke[5], Albert Ruhakana[6]

Introduction

The topographic and orographic characteristics of water catchments are key factors disadvantaging farmers living upstream in accessing water resources while their downstream counterparts enjoy plenty of water. Climate change is another threat to water availability for farming and poverty alleviation in rural areas. Finally, the absence of market outlets locks these farmers out of business opportunities.

In response to these issues, the Government of Kenya (GoK) introduced several pro-poor schemes enabling stakeholder participation in the management of their water resources to ensure water equity and poverty alleviation. This chapter evaluates the strengths and weaknesses of the Green Water Saving (GWS) schemes implemented in Muooni Catchment in Kenya. It focuses on the results of the Political, Economic, Social, Technological, Legal and Ecological (PESTLE) and Strengths, Weaknesses, Opportunities and Threats (SWOT) analyses of Kauti Irrigation Water Users' Association (Kauti IWUA) and presents findings based on the responses of 101 farmers and 20 key informants and a Focus Group Discussion (FGD).

The results reveal that Kauti IWUA has a high potential for curbing floods and ensuring water equity under conditions of drought. However, its weak institutional, financial and technological capacities are major barriers to achieving environmental sustainability. The latter was underscored by the lack of proper strategic plans and a disaster preparedness system as well as the obsolescence of

---

1. Corresponding Author: Dr Cush Ngonzo Luwesi. Email: C.Luwesi@cgiar.org
   Focal Region Manager, CGIAR Research Programme on Water, Land and Ecosytems (WLE) – Volta-Niger, IWMI-West Africa Office, CSIR Campus, PMB CT 112, Cantonments, Accra, Ghana
2. Senior Researcher, Department of Zoology, National Museums of Kenya, PO Box 40658-00100, Nairobi, Kenya
3. Assistant Lecturer, Department of Community and Development Studies, South Eastern Kenya University, PO Box 170-90200, Kitui, Kenya
4. Assistant Director, Climate Change Response Programme, Kenya Forest Service, PO Box 30513-00100, Nairobi, Kenya
5. Lecturer, Department of Environment and Resource Studies, University for Development Studies, PO Box 520 Wa Campus, Ghana
6. Researcher, Department of Natural Resource Management, Rwanda Agriculture Board, P.O. Box 5016 Kigali, Rwanda

the hydro-meteorological equipment. The findings of this evaluation can assist with the further implementation of the water sector reforms enshrined in the Kenya Constitution 2010.

Purpose of the Study

Climate change has been blamed for segregating rich and poor people in most rural areas in Africa, owing to its adverse effects on their livelihoods (Bates et al. 2008). In response to these climate risks and impacts, GoK introduced several pro-poor schemes to enable farmer participation in the management of natural resources and to achieve poverty alleviation (K'akumu 2008; Luwesi and Bader 2013).

In assessing the strengths and weaknesses of the GWS schemes implemented in Muooni Catchment by Kauti IWUA, the study revealed both farmer vulnerability and capability vis-à-vis water stresses in these Arid and Semi-Arid Lands (ASALs). The study particularly focused on the risks facing farmers as well as the strategies they put in place to mitigate the effects of environmental degradation on water availability and farming production under fluctuating rainfall regimes.

By focusing on the strengths and weaknesses of GWS schemes, the study will advance existing knowledge on pro-poor schemes. This will help to enhance farm profitability and foster the financial and economic viability of farmers in both on-farm and off-farm activities.

Literature Review

Climate Change and Water Inequality

Climate change is a great threat to environmental sustainability, economic development and social welfare in our global society (Field et al. 2012). Several climate scenarios predict that unprecedented natural disasters arising from social and economic changes and environmental changes will have lasting effects on community livelihoods at local, regional and global scales (Hulme et al. 2001; Pachauri 2004). Africa is especially vulnerable in as much as many rural communities, living with limited resources, depend on rainfed agriculture and livestock keeping for their livelihood (FAO 1995a).

Moreover, the changing effect of land use/cover change on hydrology is further exacerbated by global warming, resulting in increased mean surface temperatures and unpredictable rainfall patterns (FAO 1995b; UNEP 2009). This is evidenced by the cycle of El Niño (flooding) and La Niña (drought) experienced every decade in Kenya since the 1980s (Shisanya 1990; Shisanya et al. 2011). This perturbation of rainfall constitutes a major constraint on agricultural development and crop yield, with some areas being more vulnerable than others owing to the topographic and orographic characteristics of water catchments (FAO 2003; UNEP 2002; WRI 2003). These factors disadvantage many farmers living upstream in terms of access to water resources while their downstream counterparts enjoy plentiful water (Ngonzo et al. 2010). There is thus a need for "business not as usual" in the management of water resources (Berntell 2008). An Integrated Watershed Management (IWM) system is proposed to correct the differences in water use, water rights and accessibility that often result in "water inequality" (Cosgrove and Rijsberman 2000; Biswas 2004). Successful conservation of water catchments requires effective management of water at source, its equitable allocation and its efficient use by farmers (Luwesi 2011).

Pro-Poor Schemes in Response to Water Inequality

Besides facing "water inequality," most farmers in the tropics have to contend with poor incomes, not only because of poor yields but also because of the absence of market outlets and hence of business opportunities (FAO 2003). Moreover, the market provides misleading information to economic decision-makers at all levels by failing to reflect the full costs of goods and services (Brown 2001).

Effective farming resource management and decision-making should consider both endogenous and exogenous factors pertaining to agricultural production and resource allocation, use and management (Al-Salaymeh et al. 2011). Sound management of endogenous factors tends to maximise business strengths and minimise its weaknesses, while that of exogenous factors, both social and environmental, may present business opportunities that may lead to effective conservation of resources and prevent disastrous threats to their management (Waswa 2006; Boseman and Phatok 1989).

Hence, in responding to climate change and its repercussions for water, GoK introduced several reforms to the Water Act 2002, paving the way for pro-poor schemes (Mogaka et al. 2006; K'akumu 2008). These were intended to enable farmers to participate in the planning, development, allocation, management, monitoring and evaluation of water resources for poverty alleviation (WRMA 2010). Novel schemes have recently been developed based on the premise that there are cause-effect relationships between land use/cover changes, ecological functions and community welfare (Luwesi and Bader 2013). They include Payments for Watershed Services (PWS), Green Water Credits (GWC), Clean Development Mechanisms (CDM), and Reducing Emissions from Deforestation and forest Degradation (REDD+) (Luwesi et al. 2012; Akombo et al. 2014).

These schemes enable community members, water services providers and development partners to pay for watershed services that are provided by local stakeholders in a well-defined and voluntary transaction. The aim is to secure the sustainability of the services, provided the stakeholders continue to supply these services (conditionality) (Wunder 2005). These schemes actually result in benefits that would not have been provided without payment. These payments in cash or kind, including governmental duties, result in invaluable environmental services provided to local stakeholder and the government (Jumbe and Angelsen 2011). Above all, these pro-poor schemes have been found to be effective mechanisms initiated by local stakeholders for poverty alleviation in place of national poverty reduction strategies (Hardner and Rice 2002). They are well suited to ensuring sustainable farming management in times of water stress and scarcity (Luwesi and Bader 2013).

However, some scholars are sceptical about the ability of such schemes to generate valuable environmental services (Achard et al. 2002; Balmford et al. 2002). One reason is that degradation continues, despite billions of dollars invested in stemming the global loss of native ecosystems (Pattanayak and Kramer 2001; Pattanayak and Wendland 2007). This rapid ecosystems' degradation may be partly attributed by the fact that many of the environmental services supplied are by nature externalities (Arrow et al. 2000). Consequently, communities implementing these pro-poor schemes have failed to create institutions that internalise the public values of intact ecosystems (Pattanayak et al. 2010). Finally, Shisanya et al. (2014) argue that GWS schemes are at a crossroads in the ASALs of Kenya because they are not financially and economically feasible, despite being environmentally, politically and socially innovative. This chapter presents empirical results that enhance our understanding of the pro-poor schemes adopted in Kenyan ASALs and their strengths and weaknesses in curbing climate change impacts and assuring farmers' livelihoods.

Methodology
Study Area
Muooni Catchment is a small catchment area located in south-eastern Kenya, within Machakos County, Kathiani Division and Mitaboni Location. It is 25 km² large and lies between latitudes 1.24 °S and 1.28 °S, and longitudes 37.16 °E and 37.20 °E (Figure 1). It is dry and hilly area, with altitudes of 1,434 (near Kathiani) to 2,005 metres (at Mutondoni) above sea level. The catchment is part of Upper Midland Agro-Ecological Zone 4 (UM4-AEZ), a zone of medium potential and suitable for sunflowers and maize. The land is intensively cultivated, even the steep slopes. Yet, its climate is not suited to such cropping, conditions ranging from arid to semi-arid (Luwesi et al. 2011).

The El Niño Southern Oscillation (ENSO) often affects agricultural production in terms of rainfed and irrigated agricultural yields and crop treatments (Jaetzold et al. 2007). That is why the short rainy season becomes either extremely wet or totally dry in the course of climate change. Mean annual rainfall ranges between 500 and 1,300 mm, with 66 % reliability and annual evapotranspiration of about 1,622 mm. Water in the catchment area is mainly supplied by Muooni River and its dam, as well as by rainfall (Table 1).

Some homesteads harvest rainwater and/or pump water directly from the

Figure 1: Muooni Catchment Area

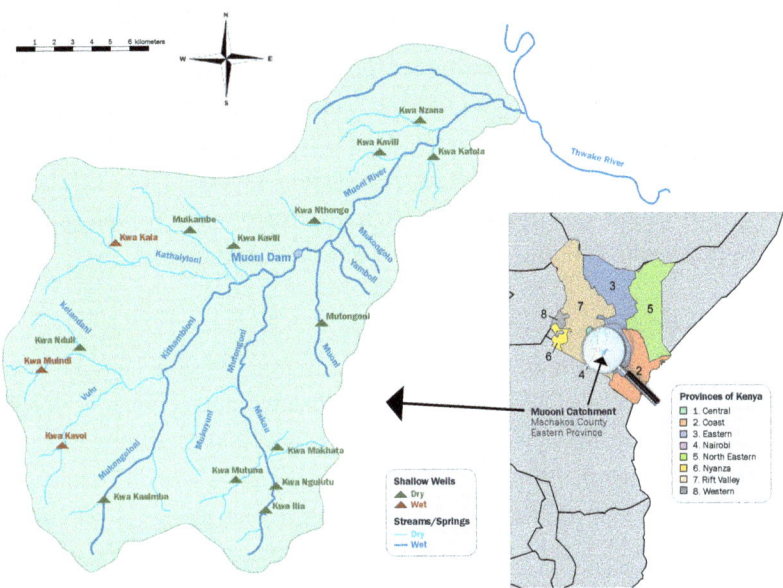

Source: Luwesi et al. (2012)

Table 1: Key hydrological features of Muooni Catchment

No	Characteristics	Values
1	Catchment area	25 km²
2	Muooni dam reservoir area	15.2 hectares
3	Annual average rainfall	~ 540 mm
4	Rainfall reliability (% Effective Rainfall)	66 %
5	Estimated evapo-transpiration	~ 1,622 mm
6	Altitude at spillway level	1614 m
7	Catchment altitude	1,434–2,005 m.
8	Average Min. temperature	12.0 °C
9	Average Max. temperature	23.0 °C
10	Average annual temperature	17.5 °C
11	Population in 2010	~ 25,000 pers.
12	Population density in 2010	~ 1,000 pers./km²
13	Total water demand in 2010	~ 842 m³/day
14	Estimated water demand by 2030	~1,800 m³/day
15	Average Muooni dam yield	~ 258.5 m³/day
16	Muooni dam specific capacity (Spillway level)	~836,000 m³/year
17	Average borehole yield	~8.64 m³/day
18	Borehole specific capacity	~451.1 m³/year
19	Average discharge during high flow	1.69 m³/ sec

Source: Luwesi et al. (2012)

dam for storage in plastic and underground tanks (Oduor 2003). Food is generally provided through agriculture, livestock-keeping and small-scale businesses. No doubt, soil erosion, water stress and food insecurity are major concerns among Muooni Catchment farmers. Since 2009, the Water Resources Management Authority (WRMA) has tried to address these challenges by developing a Catchment Management Strategy (CMS) for the Athi Basin (WRMA 2010). However, a Water Resource Users' Association (WRUA) has not been established in Muooni Catchment, although an environmental management committee overseeing Muooni Dam has, as has the Kauti IWUA.

Research Design

This research was built on an explanatory design to develop causal explanations between the effect of GWS schemes on environmental services at one end and the effect of farming water availability on farmers' profitability and welfare at the other (Krathwoh 1998). The explanatory design is useful for answering the "why" questions pertaining to the sustainability of pro-poor schemes in Kenyan ASALs in the course of climate change (Mugenda and Mugenda 2003). The explanation was not restricted to fact finding about Kauti IWUA but was extended to other Kenyan ASALs so as to be able to generate problem-solving strategies for farming water disasters (Kerlinger 1986).

Sampling Strategy and Data Collection

The selection of Muooni Catchment is mainly explained by the need to build scenarios of vulnerability-capability in relation to water disasters, with a focus on droughts and floods. A stratified random sampling strategy was used to select farms at Muooni Dam site. The study area was divided into two homogenous ecological strata to ease data collection, namely the Upper Sub-Catchment Area (USCA) and the Lower Sub-Catchment Area (LSCA) (Krumme 2006). The USCA was demarcated as the "green water provision area," owing to its higher altimetry (generally greater than 1 %). The LSCA was "the green water demand area," since its altimetry is normally below 1 %. The study also used the Zeiller (2000) random walk sampling technique to demarcate a total of 101 farms for survey questionnaires, 21 FGD participants and 20 key informants for in-depth interviews. These data enabled the development of a database in the Statistical Package for Social Sciences (SPSS) and MS Excel spreadsheets.

Data Analysis

Firstly, the study rated the performance of the management of Kauti IWUA to evaluate water service delivery against the targets set out in its strategic plans using an integrated PESTLE analysis and Downing (2003) Vulnerability-Capacity Assessment (VCA) (Table 2).

Table 2: Communities' response-capacity to climate disasters

	Adaptive Capacity	
Impacts	Low	High
High	Vulnerable communities	Development opportunities
Low	Residual Risks	Sustainability

Source: Adapted from Downing (2003)

The PESTLE and VCA were based on farmers' responses during the FGD and the survey as well as literary works related to the study area. Then, the study explored the best farming and watershed management practices and the failures under the GWS schemes in Muooni Catchment. SWOT analysis of these pro-poor schemes was useful for this purpose.

Results and Discussion

Key Findings from the PESTLE Analysis

The analysis estimated the contribution of the pro-poor schemes established by Kauti IWUA in supporting environmental sustainability and water equity in Muooni Catchment. Findings from the study show that Kauti IWUA performed fairly well but not as expected, owing to weak institutional capacity development (Figure 2).

Kauti IWUA had a weak institutional capacity (15.6 %) for achieving social equity, business success, economic development and environmental sustain-

Figure 2: Capability to manage drought in Muooni Catchment

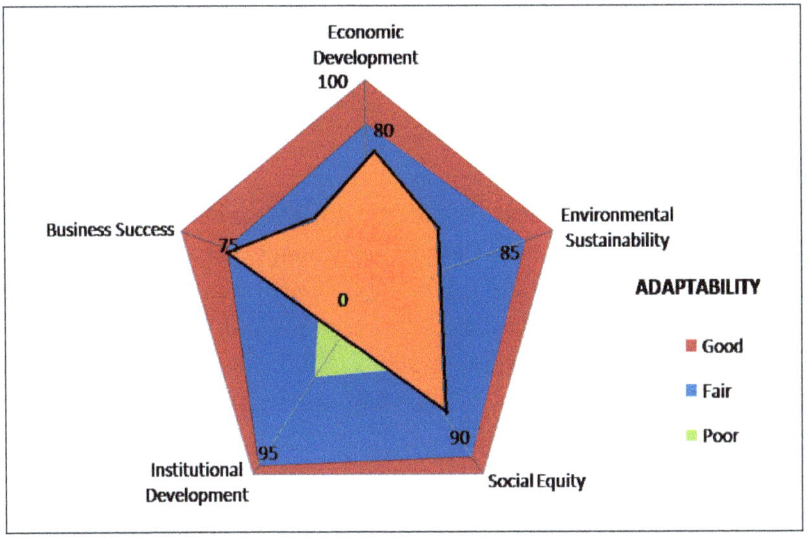

Source: Luwesi et al. (2012)
Note: The orange polygon shows Muooni's capability to manage drought.

ability. However, its pro-poor schemes did achieve high rates of social equity (75.0 %), business success (75.1 %) and economic development (68.7 %) under conditions of drought. Its adaptive capacity was rated poor with regard to ensuring environmental sustainability (37.5 %). One major weakness highlighted in the study was the fact that Kauti IWUA did not have up-to-date strategic plans to mitigate environmental disasters. However, its overall contribution to social welfare and economic development in Muooni Catchment was rated fair (54.4 %) under changing climatic conditions. These results were later validated by the SWOT analysis.

Nonetheless, global and local climate warming will remain a serious threat to the management of Muooni Catchment. It will be accompanied by the risks of wildfire and water salination inherent in La Niña droughts (Leah et al, 2014). Risks of water-related conflicts could also escalate (Besada and Werner, 2015), along with waterborne diseases and plant, livestock and human mortality (McMichael, 2012) under conditions of severe water scarcity.

In such circumstances, farmers will face very low returns on investment and water supplies. Unfortunately, they have very weak capacity to write bankable proposals (or afford consultancy fees) in applying for grants. Further, they are unable to provide collateral for borrowing money from commercial banks and other private institutions. This is in part attributed to the lack of government backing for sovereign guarantees and insufficient motivation among bankers to design banking products tailored to the needs of smallholder farms. Thus, farmers need to diversify their financing sources alongside savings, borrowing and grant lending. Innovative financing mechanisms for farmers may encompass such pro-poor schemes as microfinance, Build-Operate-Lend (BOL), Build-Operate-Sell (BOS) or Build-Operate-Transfer (BOT), and other PPPs (Preston 1997; Luwesi 2011).

Key Findings from the SWOT and VCA Analyses

The study was interested in strategies used by farmers to mitigate the effects of land degradation and water stress. The SWOT analysis mainly focused on the three hydro-climatic components relevant to Muooni Catchment: (i) flood severity; (ii) nocturnal warming; and (iii) drought severity.

First, the analysis acknowledged farmers' use of Soil and Water Conservation (SWC) measures and Early Warning Systems (EWS) (Tiffen and Mortimore 2002). These helped to prevent and subdue high surface runoff and flash floods (Plate 1).

However, some of the SWC measures were inconsistent with soil and water conservation owing to excessive multiple cropping, the planting of eucalyptus trees in wetlands and widespread open furrows, among other factors. Among the weaknesses stressed in this study, Muooni Catchment was lacking a proper

Plate 1: Soil erosion and soil conservation measures around Muooni Dam

strategy for disaster mitigation, besides having weak technological capacity due to the obsolescence of the hydro-meteorological equipment. These weaknesses may have been compounded threats such as El Niño flash floods, high erosion and the risk of mass movements, water siltation and pollution. Weak enforcement of the Water Act 2002 by public officers and the absence of a formal institution mandated to manage the catchment were among the sources of this catchment's degradation. However, local stakeholders could have tapped the opportunities arising from local legislation and policies, institutions, strategies, plans and other disaster risk-management tools. The latter include improved farming technologies implemented in Kenya, training institutions and environmental NGOs.

Second, Kauti IWUA did not have strategic action plans focused on disaster risk reduction for the whole of Muooni Catchment. There was thus a need for training local staffers on disaster monitoring and prevention. The installation and upgrading of the existing meteorological equipment in Mitaboni and Uuni meteorological stations is also a pressing need. Finally, community sensitisation and awareness creation on climate risks and local stakeholder capacity-building on climate impact adaptation and mitigation need to be intensified.

Concerning the risks of nocturnal warming and drought severity, the SWOT analysis recognised the skills of Muooni Catchment's farmers in increasing vegetation cover and humidity by using agro-forestry and reforestation, despite their weak agronomic abilities to protect crops under water stress. There were also efficient irrigation systems introduced by Kauti IWUA. These included drip irrigation and the use of spiral or sprinkler irrigation devices. However, the analysis questioned the lack of formal coordination of catchment management, inconsistent monitoring and coordination of water withdrawals, and the very limited zero-grazing practised in the catchment.

Muooni farmers need therefore to comply with Kenyan legislation, frameworks and policies, institutions and strategies, plans and other tools for the management of natural resources at catchment level. These include the 1999 Environmental Management Coordination Act (EMCA), the Water Act 2002 and related policies and strategies. With the advice of agricultural extension officers, implementation of these legal provisions may enhance protection of forests and other public lands, and increase crop protection against water stress. This would enable carbon trading on the international market for implementation of pro-poor schemes.

The following strategic actions are recommended for the new catchment management authority: (1) to regulate, measure and charge all water uses at their abstraction or effluent discharge points; (2) to promote agronomic technologies such as greenhouses, crop selection, drought resistant plants, etc.; (3) to promote alternative farming schemes in the form of trusts and cooperatives for production, savings and credits; (4) to train farmers in PPPs, proposal writing and business literacy; (5) to train farmers in marketing strategies to enable them to explore new markets and PPP financing options and increase their investments in farming and/or in off-farm sectors.

By seizing these opportunities, farmers may be able to blend different types of financing with joint ventures for implementing GWS schemes. If some farmers feel they have reached a point of no-return, they may have recourse to available off-farm activities in the catchment.

Table 3 summarizes the results of these findings. Table 4 provides a key for the interpretation of the SWOT matrix.

Discussion of Key Findings

There is no doubt that farmers are more vulnerable to drought than flooding in Eastern Kenya. This can be attributed to the high risk of changing hydro-climatic conditions triggered by ill-planned land-use activities and subsequent environmental changes (Heurtefeux et al. 2011). The latter are linked to global warming and rising sea surface temperatures, ocean currents and atmospheric winds in the southern hemisphere commonly known as El Niño (flood) and La Niña (drought) (Jaetzold et al. 2007; McGray et al. 2007). These factors impact farmland productivity and sedimentation of water channels (Terer 2004). However, since individual farmer's capability will guide their future adaptation to water disasters, instead of their resource endowments. Unfortunately, they badly lack such capacities as well as community integration, which are key for preparedness for future disasters in Muooni Catchment (Pelling 2004; Berg 2007; Mukheibir 2008). This includes the ability of local stakeholders to initiate PPPs and build strong institutions to ensure that water is available to all equitably in normal times as well as in situations of stress (Miller et al. 1997; Adgar 2000; Agrawal and Perrin 2008).

Table 3: Consolidated SWOT Analysis for interventions in Muooni

Climate Factor	Strengths	Weaknesses	Opportunities	Threats	Strategic Actions
Flood Severity	S_1, S_2, S_3	W_1, W_2, W_3	O_1, O_2, O_3	T_1, T_2, T_3, T_4	Kauti IWUA to design a strategic action plan for disaster mitigation in Muooni Catchment Train its staff in disaster monitoring and prevention Install new hydro-meteorological stations/upgrade existing equipment Intensify sensitisation meetings and awareness-creation campaigns on climate change and water conservation
Nocturnal Warming	$S_1, S_2, S_3, S_4, S_5, S_6$	$W_1, W_3, W_4, W_5, W_6, W_7, W_8$	$O_1, O_2, O_3, O_4, O_5, O_6, O_7$	$T_1, T_2, T_3, T_4, T_5, T_6, T_7, T_8, T_9$	Intensify sensitisation on the use of effective agronomic technologies for soil/water conservation (i.e., mulching, tillage, greenhouses, crop selection, drought resistant plants, etc.) Kauti IWUA to introduce in situ demonstrations to upgrade farmers' knowledge Promote the use of zero-grazing WRMA Office in Machakos to initiate public consultations for the creation of a WRUA that will coordinate overall catchment management WRMA to map all water resources and demarcate them, from protected forests and other public lands as well as settlements WRUA to implement participatory approaches for water resource allocation and management by involving all relevant institutions WRUA to create awareness of the water sector reforms
Drought Severity	$S_1, S_2, S_3, S_4, S_5, S_6, S_7, S_8, S_9, S_{10}, S_{11}$	$W_1, W_3, W_4, W_5, W_6, W_7, W_8, W_9, W_{10}, W_{11}, W_{12}, W_{13}$	$O_1, O_2, O_3, O_4, O_6, O_7, O_8, O_9, O_{10}, O_{11}$	$T_1, T_2, T_3, T_4, T_5, T_6, T_7, T_8, T_9, T_{10}, T_{11}, T_{12}$	The new WRUA to regulate, measure and charge all water users at their abstraction points or effluent discharge points by setting meters and tariffs Train farmers on PPPs and proposal writing. Promote alternative farming schemes in the form of production, savings and credit trusts and cooperatives Farmers to explore new markets and Public Private Partnership financing options (grants, lending, microfinance, BOL, BOS, BOT) Promote agronomic technologies such as greenhouses, crop selection, drought-resistant plants, etc. Increase investments in off-farm sectors Train farmers in business literacy

Source: Luwesi et al. (2012)

Table 4: Key to the consolidated SWOT matrix [1]

Climate factors	SWOT Labels	S, W, O and T Assessed
Flood Severity	Strengths	S_1: Terraces, contours and runoff cutouts to mitigate storm intensity/soil erosion S_2: Existing hydro-meteorological stations in Mitaboni and Uuni S_3: Use of early warning systems for disaster prevention
	Weaknesses	W_1: No formal strategy and plan for mitigating disaster at catchment level W_2: Weak technological capacity/obsolescent hydro-meteorological equipment W_3: Inconsistent farming methods with soil and water conservation (i.e., excessive multiple cropping, planting eucalyptus in wetlands, multiple open furrows, etc.)
	Opportunities	O_1: Disaster management legislation and policies, institutions, strategies, plans and tools for implementation O_2: Improved agro-technologies O_3: Existing training institution and NGOs
	Threats	T_1: El Niño flood destruction T_2: High risk of soil erosion and mass movements T_3: Water siltation and pollution T_4: Weak public officer enforcement capability
Nocturnal Warming	Strengths	S_4: Agro-forestry and reforestation to increase vegetation cover and humidity S_5: Existing efficient irrigation systems like drip, sprinkler and spiral irrigation S_6: Existing Kauti irrigation scheme water users' association (Kauti IWUA)
	Weaknesses	W_4: Weak agronomic abilities W_5: Inefficient crop protection under water stress W_6: Limited use of zero-grazing W_7: Lack of a formal water institutions to coordinate catchment management W_8: Lack of consistent monitoring and coordination of water withdrawal points
	Opportunities	O_4: Existing legal provisions for the protection of forests and other public lands O_5: Existing agricultural extension services O_6: Possibility of trading carbon on the international market O_7: Existing national legislation, frameworks and policies, institutions, strategies, plans and tools for implementation at the catchment level
	Threats	T_5: Catchment warming T_6: Risk of wildfire emergencies and water salination T_7: La Niña droughts T_8: High risk of escalation of water-related conflicts T_9: High risk of waterborne diseases T_{10}: High mortality risk for plants, livestock and humans due to water scarcity
Drought Severity	Strengths	S_7: Efficient hydropolicies (rainwater harvesting and storage in tanks and dams) S_8: Existing water dam at Isyukoni S_9: Existing water treatment plant in Kathiani S_{10}: Use of mulching and tillage S_{11}: Use of zero-grazing, organic and mineral fertilisers to enrich the soil
	Weaknesses	W_9: Lack of measuring devices for charging water abstractions and charging W_{10}: Lack of motivation to initiate Public Private Partnership (PPP) schemes W_{11}: Weak capacity to write proposals, afford consultancy fees and collaterals W_{12}: Limited use of crop/plant selection and greenhouses to adapt to drought W_{13}: Low returns on investments in farming and water supply
	Opportunities	O_8: Availability of governmental support and development partnersfunding for developing technical skills and improving the balance sheet O_9: Existing banking loans and private investors' joint ventures O_{10}: Availability of rentable off-farm activities O_{11}: Existing facilities and basic infrastructure for implementing GWS schemes
	Threats	T_{11}: Lack of motivation from bankers to offer banking products tailored to smallholder farmers T_{12}: Lack of government backing and sovereign guarantees allowing farmers access to diversified sources of funding.

Source: Luwesi et al. (2012)

Conclusion and Recommendations

This study has built a case based on the assumption that proper planning skills and the capacity to convert management tools into results are some of the abilities pro-poor schemes should consider to enable future adaptation by farmers to water disasters. Farmers living in Muooni Catchment and Kauti area in particular have a high potential to curb floods but greater vulnerability in controlling drought. Kauti IWUA has introduced innovative and efficient pro-poor schemes that perform fairly well. The analysis, however, questioned the lack of formal coordination of catchment management, which is a major cause of farmer vulnerability to water stress and scarcity. This was mainly evident in the lack of a proper strategy for disaster reduction and weak technological capacity, basically due to the obsolescence of the hydro-meteorological equipment as well as a weak financial capacity.

This study recommends that Kauti IWUA develops strategies focused on farmers' capability to manage water resources effectively and distribute them equitably to all. This will determine their future adaptation to droughts and/or floods. Though the continuous use of SWC measures and EWS remains an asset for preventing and mitigating high surface runoff and flash floods, farming practices inconsistent with soil and water conservation need to be discouraged. In that vein, crops and trees that support water infiltration and pollinator diversity can assist farmers in achieving food security and wood fuel sufficiency while sustaining water in the catchment. This would also enable farmers to take advantage of carbon trading on the international market to foster green water saving. These findings may shed light on further implementation of the water sector reforms in Muooni in line with the Kenya Constitution 2010.

Key Policies and Research Implications

Kauti IWUA needs to develop strategies that will unleash farmers' capability to manage water resources effectively and distribute them equitably to all. This study has built a response-capability case and found that pro-poor schemes need proper planning skills and the capacity to convert management tools into results. For sustainability, government policies need to focus on building watershed management institutions that enhance farmers' adaptability to water disasters. Farmers living in Muooni Catchment in general and Kauti area in particular ought to sharpen their adaptive capacities and skills in curbing drought impacts. For that reason, scientific research will have positive feedback on policy-making if innovative and efficient pro-poor schemes that perform fairly well are introduced in Muooni Catchment, Kauti area in particular. Such schemes will enable not only formal coordination of catchment management but also address the root causes of farmers' vulnerability to water stress and scarcity.

The GoK also needs to design proper strategic policies that focus on drought

Disaster Risk Reduction (DRR) based on technological innovation, meteorological information and sustained financial capacity. It should basically tackle the issue of the obsolescence of hydro-meteorological equipment, Early Warning Systems (EWS) as well as the weak financial capacity of most farmer organisations. Researchers ought to find how to blend microfinance with successful GWS schemes to enable smallholders to be eligible for borrowing and other banking facilities. Extension organisations and other social public services run by government as well as group formations, development organisations and private enterprises will need to get involved in the whole process in order to build farmers' capacity to increase GWS schemes' financial viability and efficiency through effective PPPs. Finally, the development of participatory approaches to planning, allocation, monitoring and evaluation of all resources in the catchment and irrigation in particular should be a priority in achieving water equity in farming in Muooni Catchment and Kauti area.

References

Achard, F., H. Eva, H. Stibig, P. Mayaux, J. Gallego, T. Richards, T. and J. Malingreau (2002) "Determination of deforestation rates of the world's humid tropical forests." *Science* (9 August): 999–1002.

Agrawal, A. and N. Perrin (2008) Climate adaptation, local institutions and rural livelihoods. IFRI Working Paper W081-6. Michigan: University of Michigan.

Akombo, R., C. Luwesi, C. Shisanya and J. Obando (2014) "Green Water Credits for Sustainable Agriculture and Forestry in Arid and Semi-Arid Tropics of Kenya." *Journal of Agri-Food and Applied Sciences* 2(4): 86–92.

Al-Salaymeh, A., I. Al-Khatib and H. Arafat (2011) "Towards Sustainable Water Quality: Management of Rainwater Harvesting Cisterns in Southern Palestine." *Water Resources Management* 25: 1721–36.

Arrow, K., G. Daily, P. Dasgupta, S. Levin, K. Maler, E. Maskin, D. Starrett, T. Sterner and T. Tietenberg (2000) "Managing ecosystem resources." *Environment, Science and Technology* 34: 1401–06.

Balmford, A., A. Bruner, P. Cooper, R. Costanza, S. Farber, R. Green, M. Jenkins, P. Jefferiss, V. Jessamy, J. Madden, K. Munro, N. Myers, S. Naeem, J. Paavola, M. Rayment, S. Rosendo, J. Oughgarden, K. Trumper and R. Turner (2002) "Economic reasons for conserving wild nature." *Science* (9 August): 950–53.

Bates, B., Z. Kundzewicz, S. Wu and J. Palutikof (eds) (2008) Climate Change and Water. Technical Paper IV of the Intergovernmental Panel on Climate Change. Geneva: IPCC Secretariat.

Berg, S. (2007) "Conflict resolution: benchmarking water utility performance." *Public Administration and Development* 27 (1): 1–11.

Berntell, A. (2008) "Getting to Business Not as Usual." *Stockholm Water Front* (April): 1–2.

Besada, H., & Werner, K. (2015). An assessment of the effects of Africa's water crisis on food security and management. *International Journal of Water Resources Development*, *31*(1), 120–133.

Biswas, A. (2004) "Integrated water resources management: A reassessment – A water forum contribution." *Water International* 29 (2): 248–56.

Boseman, G. and A. Phatok (1989) *Strategic Management: Text and Cases*. New York: Wiley.

Brown, L. (2001) *Eco-Economy: Building an economy for the earth*. New York: Norton.

Cosgrove, W. and F. Rijsberman (2000) *World Water Vision: Making Water Everybody's Business*. London: Earthscan.

Downing, T. (2003) "Linking sustainable livelihoods and global climate change in vulnerable food systems." *Die Erde* 133: 363–78.

Food and Agriculture Organization (FAO) (1995a) Water Report 7– Irrigation in Africa in figures. Rome: FAO Secretariat.

FAO- UN Food and Agriculture Organization (1995b) "Planning for Sustainable Use of Land Resources: Towards a New Approach." *FAO Land and Water Bulletin* 2: 25–46.

FAO- UN Food and Agriculture Organization (2003) *World agriculture: Towards 2015/2030 An FAO perspective*. Rome: FAO Secretariat.

Field, C.B., V. Barros, T.F. Stocker, D. Qin, D.J. Dokken, K.L. Ebi, M.D. Mastrandrea, K.J. Mach, G.-K. Plattner, S.K. Allen, M. Tignor and P.M. Midgley (eds.) (2012) *Managing the Risks of Extreme Events and Disasters to Advance Climate Change Adaptation. A Special Report of Working Groups and of the Intergovernmental Panel on Climate Change (IPCC)*. Cambridge: Cambridge University Press.

Hardner, J. and R. Rice (2002) Rethinking green consumerism. *Scientific American* (May 2002): 89–95.

Heurtefeux, H., P. Sauboua, P. Lanzellotti and A. Bichot (2011) "Coastal risk management modes: The managed realignment as a risk conception more integrated." In M. Savino (ed.) *Risk Management in Environment, Production and Economy*. Rijeka: InTech, pp 3–26.

Hulme, M., R. Doherty, T. Ngara, M. New and D. Lister (2001) "African Climate Change: 1900–2100. *Climate Research* 17: 145–68.

Jaetzold, R., H. Schmidt, B. Hornetz and C. Shisanya (2007) "Natural conditions and farm management information- Part C East Kenya, Subpart C1 Eastern Province." In: Ministry of Agriculture and German Technical Cooperation (GTZ) *Farm Management Handbooks of Kenya*, Vol. II. Nairobi, pp. 1–571.

Jumbe, C. and A. Angelsen (2006) "Do the poor benefit from devolution policies? Evidence from Malawi's forest co-management program." *Land Economics* 82(4): 562–81.

K'akumu, O. (2008) "Mainstreaming the participatory approach in water resource governance: The 2002 Water Law in Kenya." *Development* 51: 56–62.

Kerlinger, F. (1986) *Foundations of Behavioral Research* (3rd ed.) Orlando FL: Harcourt Brace.

Krathwoh, D. (1998) *Methods of Educational and Social Science Research: An Integrated Approach* (2nd ed.). New York: Longman.

Krumme, K. (2006) EFU – Ecological Functional Units: A basis for sustainable development planning. FWU Water Resources Publications, Vol. 5: 17–27.

Leigh, C., Bush, A., Harrison, E. T., Ho, S. S., Luke, L., Rolls, R. J., & Ledger, M. E. (2014). Ecological effects of extreme climatic events on riverine ecosystems: insights from Australia. *Freshwater Biology.*

Luwesi, C. (ed.) (2011) *Innovative Ways in Financing the Water Sector.* SWAP/bfz Workshop Report, 7–11 November. Mombasa: BFZ – Bavarian Finance Center and WaterCap.

Luwesi, C. and E. Bader (2013) "Essentials of Implementation of Improved Green Water Management In Muooni Catchment, Machakos District of Kenya." *Journal of Agri-Food and Applied Sciences* 1 (2): 63–70.

Luwesi, C., C. Shisanya and J. Obando (2011) "Toward a hydro-economic approach for risk assessment and mitigation planning for farming water disasters in semi-arid Kenya. In M. Savino (ed.) *Risk Management in Environment, Production and Economy.* Rijeka: InTech, pp 27–46.

Luwesi, C., C. Shisanya and J. Obando (2012) *Warming and Greening: The Dilemma Facing Green Water Economy under Changing Micro-Climatic Conditions in Muooni Catchment* (Machakos, Kenya). Saarbrücken: Lambert Academic.

McGray, H., A. Hammill, R. Bradley, E.L. Schipper and J-E. Parry (2007) *Weathering the storm: Options for framing adaptation and development.* Washington DC: World Resource Institute (WRI).

McMichael, A. J. (2012). Insights from past millennia into climatic impacts on human health and survival. *Proceedings of the National Academy of Sciences, 109*(13), 4730–4737.

Miller, K., S. Rhodes and L. Macdonnell (1997) "Water allocation in a changing climate: Institutions and adaptation." *Climate Change* 35: 157–77.

Mogaka, H., S. Gichere, R. Davis and R. Hirji (eds) (2006) Climate Variability and Water Resources Degradation in Kenya: Improving Water Resources Development and Management. World Bank Working Paper No. 69.

Mugenda, O. and A. Mugenda (2003) Research methods – Quantitative and Qualitative methods (rev ed.) Nairobi: Act Press.

Mukheibir, P. (2008) "Water resources management strategies for adaptation to climate-induced impacts in South Africa." *Water Resources Management* 22: 1259–76.

Ngonzo, C., C. Shisanya and J. Obando (2010) "Land use and water demand under a changing climate: Experiences of smallholder farmers from Muooni." In S.P. Saikia (ed.) *Climate Change.* Assam: International Book Distributors, pp. 117–40.

Oduor, A. (2003) Hydrologic Assessment of Smallholder Runoff Catchment Schemes: A Case of Harvesting Rainwater in Semi-Arid Machakos, Kenya. Delft: UNESCO International Institute for Hydraulics and Environmental Engineering.

Pachauri, R. (2004) "Climate and humanity." *Global Environment Change* 14: 101–3.

Pattanayak, S. and R. Kramer (2001) "Pricing ecological services: Willingness to pay for drought control services in Indonesia." *Water Resources Research* 37(3): 771–78.

Pattanayak, S. and K. Wendland (2007) "Nature's care: Diarrhea, watershed protection and biodiversity conservation in flores, Indonesia." *Biodiversity and Conservation* 16(10): 2801–19.

Pattanayak, S., S. Wunder and P. Ferraro (2010) "Show me the money: Do payments supply environmental services in developing countries?" *Review of Environmental Economics and Policy* 4 (2): 254–74.

Pelling, M. (2004) Social capital and institutional adaptation to climate change. Rapid Climate Change Project (RCC) Working Paper 2. Liverpool: University of Liverpool.

Preston, M. (1997) *Investing in Mountains: Innovative Mechanisms and Promising Examples for Financing Conservation and Sustainable Development*. West Virginia: Mountain Institute.

Shisanya, C. (1990) "The 1983–1984 Drought in Kenya." *Journal of Eastern African Research and Development* 20: 127–48.

Shisanya, C., C. Luwesi and J. Obando (2014) "Innovative but not feasible: Green water saving schemes at the crossroads in semi-arid lands." In OSSREA (eds) *Innovative Water Resource Use and Management for Poverty Reduction in Sub-Saharan Africa: An Anthology*. Addis Ababa: OSSREA Secretariat, pp. 137–72.

Shisanya, C., C. Recha and A. Anyamba (2011) "Rainfall Variability and Its Impact on Normalized Difference Vegetation Index in Arid and Semi-Arid Lands of Kenya." *International Journal of Geosciences* 2: 36–47.

Terer, J. (2004) *The Study of Hydrologic Characteristics and Management Practices in Agricultural River Catchments: The case of Nyorongores River Catchment, Mara River Basin, Kenya*. Nairobi: Act Press.

Tiffen, M. and M. Mortimore (2002) "Agroecosystems regaining the high ground: Reviving the Hillsides of Machakos." *World Resources 2000–2001*: 149–58.

United Nations Environment Programme (UNEP) (2002) *Success stories in the struggle against desertification: A holistic and integrated approach to environmental conservation and sustainable livelihoods*. Nairobi: UNEP Division of Environmental Policy Implementation (DEPI).

UNEP- United Nations Enviornment Programme (2009) *Kenya: Atlas of Our Changing Environment*. Nairobi: UNEP Division of Early Warning Assessment

Waswa, P. (2006) "Opportunities and Challenges for Sustainable Agricultural Land Management in Kenya." In F. Waswa, S. Otor and D. Mugendi (eds) *Environment and Sustainable Development*, Vol. 1. Nairobi: Kenyatta University, pp. 52–65.

WRI – World Resource Institute (2003) "Water resources and freshwater ecosystems Kenya. EarthTrends country profiles." Accessed on 22. 09. 2010 at http://earthtrends.wri.org/pdf_library/country_profiles/wat_cou_404.pdf

WRMA- Water Resources Management Authority (2010) Enforcement of water use charges and water quality thresholds in Kenya. Report of the WRMA Training Workshop (24–28 January). Meru: IWMNet/EU Project and German Technical Cooperation (GTZ).

Zeiller M. (2000) *Methods of socio-economic analysis of rural development*. Göttingen: Institute of Rural Development, University of Göttingen.

4. Competitive Farming Strategies and their Effect on Water Provision and Profitability among Smallholder Farms

The Case of Muooni Dam Site, Kenya

Peter Philip Wambua,[4] Cush Ngonzo Luwesi,[5] Essam O. Bader,[6] Dzigbodi A. Doke[4] Rose A. Akombo,[5] Jean-Filston Mikwa[6]*

Introduction

Agriculture is acknowledged as the oldest and most important feature of human activities, as well as the backbone of civilisations and economic development. It marks as well the transition between the primitive tribe and the industrial society (Ellis 1993). However, just like most tenuous production and survival systems, agricultural production has been frustrated and perturbed by extreme climatic events leading to farming water vulnerability (Mikwa et al. 2014). Climate change and the unsustainable use of water in marginal and dry lands of the tropics are said to be the major sources of agriculture inefficiency in sub-Saharan Africa (Rockström et al. 2009). The ever-shrinking water endowment under changing climate in Kenyan Arid and Semi-Arid Lands (ASALs) has forced farmers to adopt various strategies to survive (Rockström 2003). As a matter of fact, Luwesi (2010) demonstrated that a majority among Kenyan farmers operating in the ASALs have adopted a multiple cropping strategy, which unfortunately does not help them, owing to the increasing water cost under shortage. Thence, this strategy results into plummeting total cost of their farming activities leading to high farming annual deficits. There is therefore a need to investigate the reason why such farming strategies lead to inefficiency and unprofitability in the rainfed agriculture and the provision of irrigation water.

4.* Corresponding Author: Dr Cush Ngonzo Luwesi. Email: C.Luwesi@cgiar.org
   Lecturer, Business Administration Department, Kenyatta University, PO Box 43844-00100, Nairobi, Kenya
5. Focal Region Manager, CGIAR Research Programme on Water, Land and Ecosytems (WLE)– Volta-Niger, IWMI-West Africa Office, CSIR Campus, PMB CT 112, Cantonments, Accra, Ghana
6. Associate Professor, Faculty of Agricultural Economics, Damietta University, PO Box 34517, New Damietta Egypt
4. Lecturer, Department of Environment and Resource Studies, University for Development Studies, PO Box 520 Wa Campus, Ghana
5. Assistant Director, Climate Change Response Programme, Kenya Forest Service, PO Box 30513-00100, Nairobi, Kenya
6. Assistant Lecturer, Faculty of Agronomy, University of Kisangani, P.B. 2012 Kisangani, DR Congo

Purpose of the Study

This study sought to examine some competitive strategies used by farmers to secure higher earnings and good incomes while facing the threat of unpredicted drought. The study also investigated the effects of these farming strategies on farming water supplies and profitability. By applying optimisation inventory models the study could sense farmers' water provision from the adjustment of crop water requirements and relate them to farming water use efficiency under fluctuating rainfall regimes (Luwesi et al. 2013). In this case, the analysis had to consider the limits of farming water costs and optimum crop water requirements under fluctuating rainfall regimes and link them to specific marketing strategies, including differentiation and diversification at different magnitudes and under unexpected flood and drought events.

This business oriented approach enabled a performance evaluation of the farming water use and agricultural production within the limits of the optimum crop water requirements and costs. It indeed informed on the rationale of farmers' water-use strategies and appropriateness of alternative technologies that can be used to foster a locative, technological and scale efficiencies (Luwesi et al. 2012). Finally, by elaborating on concepts of marketing strategy and agricultural profitability, this chapter presents empirical results that contribute to our understanding of new competitive farming strategies and agronomic practices with corresponding market requirements in the course of climate change (Wind and Robertson 1983).

Review of the Field

Competitive Strategies

Cateora and Graham (1999) distinguish two elements that affect marketing strategy and profitability in any type of environment. These include (1) controllable factors, namely McCarthy's "4Ps" (Product, Price, Place and Promotion) on one hand; and (2) uncontrollable factors such as macroeconomics, market competition, politics, laws, consumer loyalty and behavioural change, and technological and environmental changes, including climate change (Baker and Start 1992). While marketing strategies mostly focus on controllable factors, the analysis of profitability often takes into account the full cost of the effects of uncontrollable factors (Reichheld and Teal 1996).

In McCarthy's marketing-mix, "P = Price" generally stands for a fair charge or fee that is competitive in the market and enables full cost recovery (Wind and Robertson 1983). "P = Product" is primarily related to the quality and quantity of goods and services. Quality refers to the contents, brands and product/service lines in relation to acceptable standards, while quantity represents the key elements stored in the goods produced or capacities devoted to supplying services (Cochoy 1998; Lusch et al. 2007). In delivering quality services, Zeithaml et al.

(1990) suggest that marketers take into account customers' perceptions and expectations, needs, practices, habits, beliefs, attitudes and values. These attributes condition customers' preferences by displaying ideas, brands or labels that are appealing and may represent the benefits accruing from consumption of the said products (Ghazali et al. 2008; Martinsen 2008). That is where "P = Place" becomes a key marketing variable for mainstreaming the administrative distribution of goods and services in various market segments. This involves the organisation of service providers (suppliers) and users (clients) into specific physical and social networks for easy communication and supply of goods and services to the market (Harris and Ogbonna 2003). Thus, "P = Place" is a prerequisite for "P = Promotion," which entails public relations, promotional activities and publicity. These techniques play a key role in the creation and re-creation of the product image in the market (Webster 2002). Companies are therefore called to effectively use communication methods to sustain the adoption of their goods and services by customers (Doyle 1992).

In their research and experience with customers, Breene and Nunes (2005) distinguished high performers from their competitors based on their consistency in constructing and maintaining a certain competitive essence. Milles and Snow (1978), however, associated successful marketing with organisational performance, which was based on adaptive strategies chosen by the management to respond to the environment. The latter were consistent with a particular configuration of technology, structure and processes that enabled firms to achieve competitive advantage. Hence, some firms were categorised as "Defenders" while others were "Analysers," "Reactors" or "Prospectors." In the same vein, Porter (1998) presents a typology of generic marketing strategies that seek long-term competitive advantage. These encompass: (1) low cost leadership; (2) differentiation strategy; and (3) a market focus strategy. A firm that engages in each generic strategy but fails to achieve any of them is "stuck in the middle." Thus, a low cost leading firm's ability to outperform its competitors depends on its ability to (1) seize opportunities arising from market trends; (2) capture and protect "unfair share" of markets; (3) capture premium pricing; and to (4) prudently create and introduce new products (Ansoff and McDonnell 1990; Donnelly 1992). Therefore, a low cost leader must have optimal production costs, low prices and high margins.

Businesses capitalise on differentiation strategies to achieve economies of scale in order to generate more incomes and help "push the frontier" of innovation through the use of technology and testing of innovative delivery channels or product diversification (McGill 2006). Convenience retailing and product diversification are some of the differentiation strategies that have been successfully and widely practised in agribusiness, as well as in the sale of most electronic products and provisional services (CGAP 2010). It is thus common among firms to make products with similar prices but often of different quality, depending on consumer preferences and the way they are likely to perceive differences in quality among companies (Wambua et al. 2014). Hence, product diversification encompasses both the production of supplementary and complementary sub-products utilising innovative technologies. Convenience retailing requires an innovative delivery channel to present the product to consumers at the most accessible locations, notably along main roads and at intersections. Finally, Pearce and Robinson (2007) noted that in pursuing a focused marketing strategy, firms with a narrow focus had lower volumes and thus less bargaining power with their suppliers.

Farming Profitability

Luwesi (2010) evaluated farming profitability in Muooni Catchment of Athi River (Kenya) using a full cost method. The study assessed how climate change affects agricultural water productivity and farming profitability under fluctuating rainfall regimes. Results indicate increased costs associated with water shortages during droughts, and the opportunity cost of saving excess water that is lost during flooding in addition to normal costs of transaction and associated opportunity costs in irrigation. Likewise, in a worldwide compendium of case studies dealing with environmental valuation, Reitbergen-McCracken and Abaza (2000) reported an evaluation of the profitability of forest plantations in the Philippines that used a replacement-cost approach. The study computed the costs of soil fertility removal, agricultural loss of earnings and irrigation system inefficacy due to soil erosion and the siltation of the dam reservoir. An opportunity cost of constructing a large non-productive sediment pool was added to the total cost to prevent the adverse effects of sedimentation. These studies recommended that farmers living in harsh climatic environments like Muooni should constantly review their cropping strategies in line with market dynamics, without disregarding their environmental costs. This will help them keeping their productive cost within their minimum efficiency scales (MES) or limit average costs (LAC) and sustain their competitive advantage and farming profitability under the Production Possibility Frontiers (PPF) (Brownlie et al. 1999).

Methodology

Study Area, Sampling Strategy and Data Collection

A survey was conducted among 101 farmers located at a radius of 100 metres around Muooni Dam. Muooni Dam is an overflow gravity dam located in a narrow part of the deep valley of the Muooni River at Isyukoni sub-location of Mitaboni location and Kathiani Division, Machakos County, Kenya. The whole catchment covers about 25 km^2, which is bounded by latitude 1.24° S and 1.28° S, and longitude 37.16° E and 37.20° E. Water in this catchment is

Figure 1: Stratification from the study area

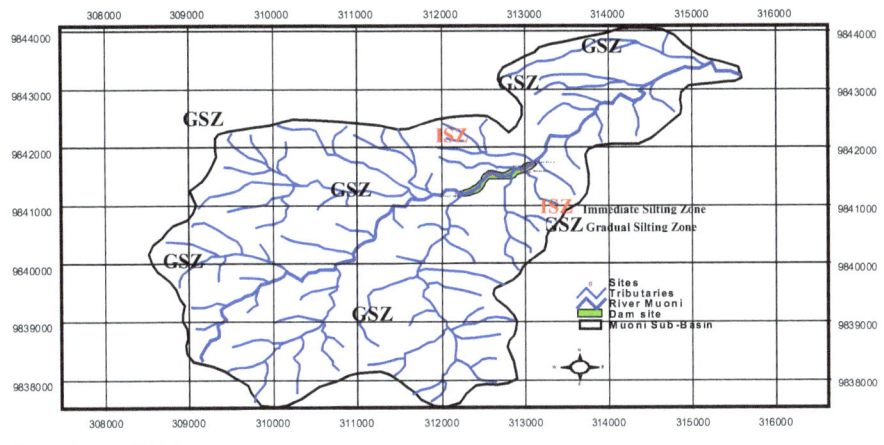

Source: Luwesi (2010)

mainly supplied by the Muooni Water Project, which totally relies on Muooni Dam (Luwesi et al. 2012).

A stratified random sampling was used to select farms at Muooni dam site. The study area was divided into two zones for easy data collection (Figure 1).

In Figure 1, Zone 1 is denoted "ISZ"(Immediate Silting Zone)of Muooni Dam due to its higher altimetry (greater than 1 %) while Zone 2 is referred to as "GSZ," "Gradual Silting Zone" because of its lower altimetry (less than 1 %). An on-farm survey was conducted within the ISZ at a radius of 100 metres around Muooni Dam and above to collect 101 questionnaire responses from farmers (Luwesi 2010). Likewise, a Focus Group Discussion (FGD) and 20 in-depth interviews took place at the GSZ to get supplementary data for the study.

It should be noted that the two hydro-ecological zones (ISZ and GSZ) were situated within one agro-ecological zone, namely the Upper Midland Agro-Ecological Zone 4 (UM4-AEZ), which is a medium potential zone suitable for sunflower and maize cropping (Jaetzold et al. 2007). This saved time and energy, as researchers avoided complications due to a wide range of farming practices in the computation of crop water requirements, farmers' water provision and the subsequent costs. An assumption was made that the prices of inputs and outputs did not vary significantly within the same AEZ.

Research Design
This research was built on an explanatory design to develop causal explanations between farmers' cropping patterns and crop evapotranspiration on one hand, and farming water supply and agricultural profitability on the other

(Krathwoh 1998; Cooper and Schindler 2001). This explanation was not only restricted to fact finding at Muooni dam site. It also included the application of important competitive marketing principles and strategies to formulate ad hoc knowledge and solutions to significant problems facing Kenyan ASALs (Kerlinger 1986). Thus, it was also useful for answering the "why" questions pertaining to current farming water productivity and farming activity sustainability in Kenyan ASALs in the course of climate change (Mugenda and Mugenda 2003).

Data Analysis

Data Pre-Processing: Data collected were first cleaned and presented in a format acceptable for processing using the Statistical Package for Social Sciences (SPSS) and MS Excel spreadsheets. This enabled the development of a database in SPSS and MS Excel that generated some 101 cases times 190 variables (from the 101 questionnaire responses), 840 cross-sectional data sets by 14 variables (from the 20 key informants interviewed) and 294 cross-sectional data sets by 14 variables (from the 21 FGD participants).

Techniques of Data Processing: Data analysis was supported by optimisation inventory models applied by Luwesi et al. (2013). These models enabled adjustment of crop water requirements in each farm under fluctuating rainfall regimes in Muooni Catchment. The study first derived crop water requirements (W_c) from "Virtual water values" (VWV) as follows:

$$W_c = \sum ETP_c \qquad \text{(Formula 1)}$$

Where,

ETP_c equals the total crop water evapotranspiration (in m³) during crop growth computed from FAO (2008) reference crop evapotranspiration (ET_m), in kg/m³, as follows:

$$ETP_c = \frac{1}{ET_m} \times Y_c \qquad \text{(Formula 2)}$$

Where,

Y_c is the total crop yield (in kg)

An incremental analysis was then conducted to derive farmers' water supply that meets crop water requirements using a theoretical water supply turnover (r). The latter was hypothesised to be equal to the ratio of the dam's active water storage capacity for a specific year by the median capacity (s_{me}), namely for 1988 (under flooding scenario or ANOR), 2008 (under a normal rainfall regime scenario or NOR) and 2020 (under a drought scenario or BNOR). Farmers' water supplies under each rainfall regime were computed as EOQ (Economic Order Quantity) for ANOR, LAC (Limit Average Cost) for NOR and MES (Minimum Efficient Scale) for BNOR using the following optimised water supply model (W_f):

$$\overline{W_f} = \overline{r} \, W_c \qquad \text{(Formula 3)}$$

Where,

$\overline{r}$ an optimised water supply turnover with the following values:

Under the NOR scenario:

$$\overline{r}_{no} = \sqrt{2q/Q} \qquad \text{(Formula 4)}$$

Under ANOR scenario:

$$\overline{r}_{an} = \sqrt{2q/(2Q-q)} \qquad \text{(Formula 5)}$$

Under BNOR scenario:

$$\overline{r}_{bn} = \sqrt{2} \qquad \text{(Formula 6)}$$

Where,

Q and q are farming activity's output and input, respectively standardised using the relations:

$$Y = P.W_c/n.Q \qquad \text{(Formula 7)}$$

$$E = P.W_c/n.q \qquad \text{(Formula 8)}$$

Where,

Y = the seasonal farming income

E = the seasonal farming expenditure

P = the shadow water price per m^3

This analysis enabled us to compute optimised crop water requirements that farmers needed to apply to keep their farming production within the limits of their irrigation water-use efficiency. It also elicited the effects of climate change on farmers' competitive strategies, which in turn affected their irrigation water provision and farming profitability.

Results and Discussion

Key Findings

Results show that Muooni farmers used inefficient competitive strategies that did not consider the limits of their farming water costs and optimum crop water requirements under fluctuating rainfall regimes. Product diversification was probably the most important competitive strategy used by farmers at different magnitudes. Farmers have adopted multiple cropping of about nine (9) seasonal crops and six (6) perennial crops on parcels as small as one (1) acre.

Figure 2 reveals that most farmers had a high preference for maize and cowpeas, mainly because they are ingredients of the traditional meal known as *Muthokoi*, and have a large share in the local market. Cassava, French beans, Irish and sweet potatoes were also important food crops grown at Muooni dam site. However, the main perennial crops grown in the study area were banana, avocado, coffee, mangoes and sugarcane (Figure 3).

Product diversification was prompted by the escalation of crop failures under unexpected drought conditions, which resulted in higher water demands and lower supplies. Market segmentation, convenience retailing and low cost-leadership competitive strategies were inappropriate in these ASALs of Kenya.

Figure 2: Subsistence food crops grown at Muooni dam site

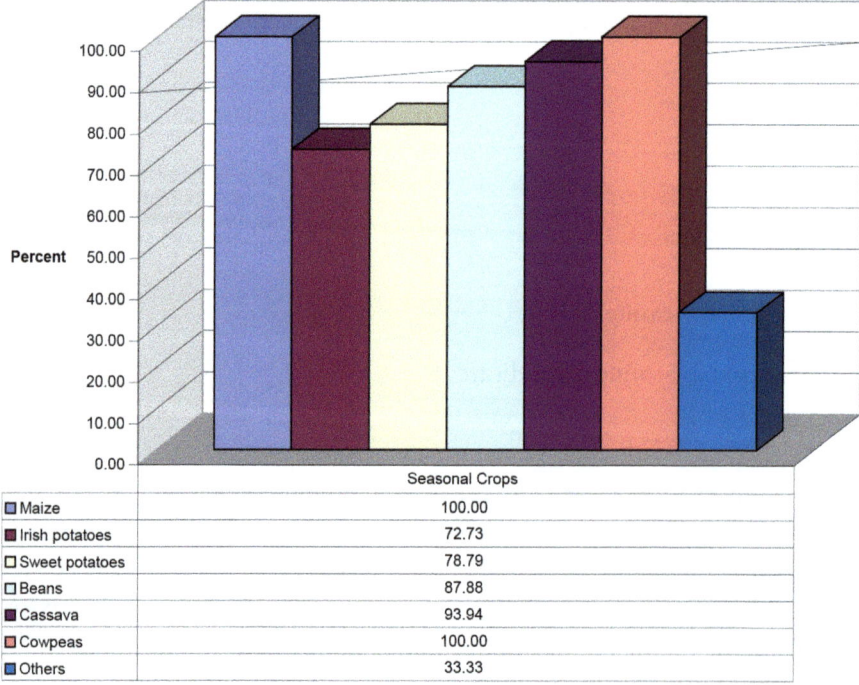

	Seasonal Crops
☐ Maize	100.00
■ Irish potatoes	72.73
☐ Sweet potatoes	78.79
☐ Beans	87.88
■ Cassava	93.94
☐ Cowpeas	100.00
■ Others	33.33

Source: Luwesi (2010)

Figure 3: Main perennial crops grown at Muooni dam site

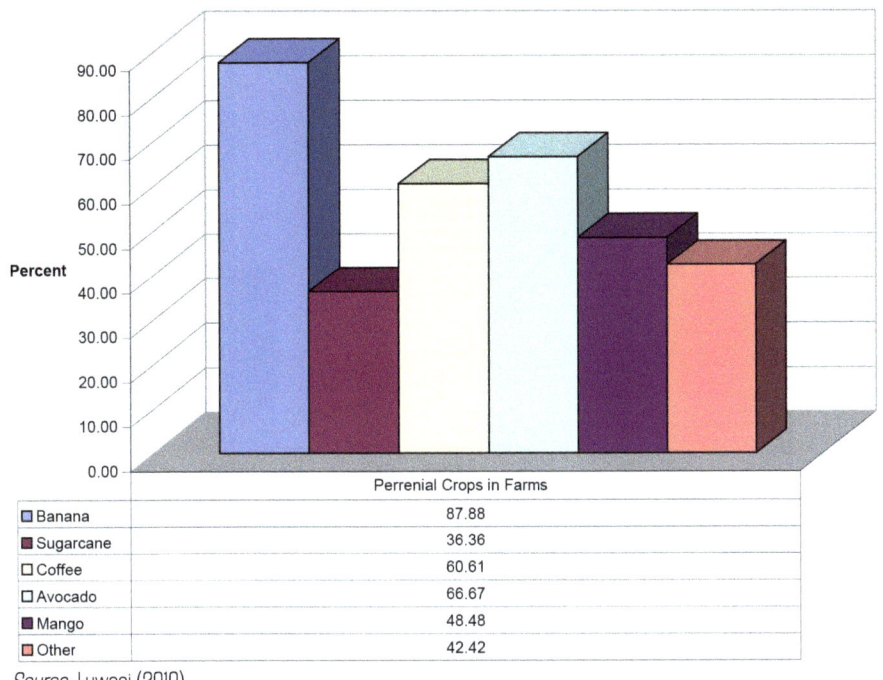

Source: Luwesi (2010)

Table 1 displays high discrepancies between farming water supplies and crop water requirements in 2010 in Muooni Catchment. Farming water in Muooni represented only 3 % of annual crop water requirements in 2010. This was an indicator of the vulnerability to low rainfall and droughts in the absence of a GWS scheme.

This overcropping strategy led to increased farming water-shortage costs and decreasing farming water productivity with plummeting total farming costs and deficits (Figure 4).

Figure 4 presents increasing farming water demands vis-à-vis decreasing water supplies and related productivity in Muooni catchment area in 2010 and the projected year 2030 under different rainfall scenarios. Luwesi (2010) reported

Table 1: Farmers' water provision and crop water requirements in Muooni (2010)

Variable		Value
Annual farmers' water provision (m³)	(1)	709.35
Annual crop water requirement (m³)	(2)	23,404.14
Gap (m³)	(3)=(2)−(1)	22,694.79
Percentage Gap (%)	(4)=100*(3)/(2)	96.97%

Source: Luwesi et al. (2012)

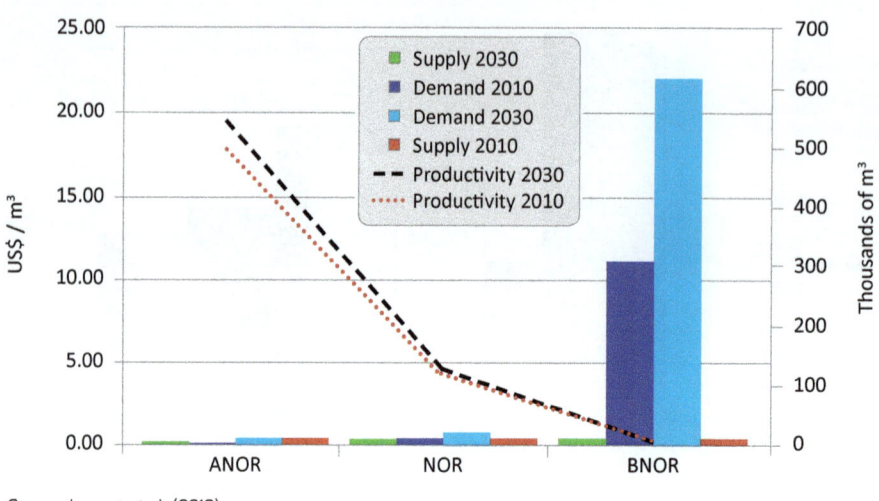

Figure 4: Farming water supply and productivity in Muooni under fluctuating regimes

Source: Luwesi et al. (2012)

that on average, Muooni farmers recorded annual deficits of US$ 529.94 for a total income of US$ 640.99 in the year 2010. The economic viability of these smallholder farms was threatened by higher average water costs of US$ 217.78 (representing 31 cents/m³) with water over-abstraction of about 231.73 m³/acre. Even though the analysis lauded Muooni farmers for their efficient hydro-policies such as Rain Water Harvesting and Storage (RWHS) and water treatment, it did not condone them for not using appropriate bylaws and tariffs to regulate water abstraction and use, along with technological devices (meters) to measure water abstractions and charge for them accordingly.

Discussion of Key Findings

Competitive farming strategies in the ASALs of Kenya are informed by the agro-ecology of the area in terms of both rainfed and irrigated agriculture and crop treatment. This chapter has shown that most farmers practise irrigation for commercial and/or subsistence agriculture using Muooni dam water. Yet the catchment area receives less than 1,000 mm of mean annual rainfall. Consequently, Muooni catchment is not likely favourable for intensive irrigation and rainfed agriculture. However, subsistence farmers do not hesitate to grow, on a small acre, maize mixed with French beans, potatoes and banana; or sorghum with cowpeas, sweet potatoes, arrow roots and pumpkins; or else millet with cassava, yams, and sugarcane. Commercial farmers stick to coffee or tea associated with horticulture and some agro-forestry, especially eucalyptus, pine and grevilia species.

Regarding crop treatments, Waswa (2006) noted that in tropical rural agrosystems food insecurity, poverty and land degradation are closely interrelated. No wonder that staple maize crop yields were extremely low in Machakos and Makueni Districts due to poor farming and unfavourable climate. Both low fertility soils and climate change make smallholder agriculture a risky enterprise in much of the two districts. There is an urgent need for farmers to increase micronutrients in these deficient soils to address the soil infertility and food shortages in this area.

When it comes to the area's climatology, Jaetzold et al. (2007) observed that agricultural water and land-use in Eastern Kenya is always affected by the El Niño Southern Oscillation (ENSO). Short rainy seasons are either extremely wet or totally dry, leading either to high soil moisture and cool climates on the top of hills, and drylands on plains and plateaus. Hence, hilltops become favourable for cropping wheat, maize and pyrethrum, but these crops tend to fail due to the shortness of the rainy season and small size of farming areas. Farming incomes there are supplemented by the growing of potatoes, coffee (in altitudes ranging from 1,650 to 1,800 m), early maturing sorghum and foxtail millet, and "marginal crops" (like Tepary beans and Tohono Z16 maize), most of the time associated with livestock farming. However, these activities have resulted in excessive water abstraction from the dam and its river as well as erosive processes and mass movement across the catchment. Notwithstanding the fact that a majority among farmers practise soil conservation measures, soil erosion around Muooni dam site is nonetheless said to be the primary cause of siltation of the dam reservoir (Luwesi et al. 2011; Ngonzo et al. 2013). The ultimate effect of soil loss from farms is reduced farming land and water productivity, and increased farming deficits, food shortage and desertification.

Conclusion and Recommendations

Competitive farming strategies are context-based, in line with market dynamics and environmental changes. Farmers operating around Muooni dam site were misusing product diversification to adjust their irrigation water provision to increased water prices without taking into consideration the available water resource. Hence, they recorded very low farming water productivity and high agricultural deficits owing to their misinterpretation of agro-ecological practices, both in terms of crop treatment and crop water requirements. The lower farming water productivity and higher agricultural deficits were exacerbated by high rates of fertile soil loss associated with farmland sub-division, over-cropping, eucalyptus tree planting and soil erosion problems that enhanced water stress in the catchment and the total cost of farming water. Farmers were thus obliged to adjust their irrigation water provision to increased water prices and higher perennial crop water requirements without taking into consideration the depleting water resources (rainfall). The widening gap between soil moisture and crop water requirements led to massive crop failures, lower farming water productivity and higher agricultural deficits in the course of climate change.

Muooni farmers need to constantly review their competitive farming strategies in line with market dynamics, without disregarding the environment in which they operate, if their competitive advantage is to be sustained within their farming Production Possibility Frontiers (PPF). Efficient farming strategies should be implemented within the limits of water costs and optimum crop water requirements under any rainfall regime. Farmers may opt for either an EOQ, or for a farming water supply adapted to the LAC or at least a Minimum Efficient Scale. This may enable farmers operating in ASALs in general, and at Muooni dam site in particular, to implement rational farming water-use strategies and appropriate alternative technologies to foster total agricultural economic efficiency. They should also adopt efficient hydro-policies, appropriate bylaws, tariffs and technologies to regulate water abstraction and use, measure water withdrawals at source and charge for them accordingly, if allocative technological and scale efficiencies are to be fostered within their farming PPF.

Key Policies and Research Implications

Competitive farming strategies are context-based, in line with the environmental changes and market dynamics. Findings arising from this study reveal that farmers' misinterpretation of agro-ecological practices and misuse of product diversification led to soil erosion problems and enhanced water stress. These were associated with farmland sub-divisions, over-cropping and water over-abstraction by eucalyptus trees. Therefore, GoK needs to create an environment that is conducive to equitable water distribution. It should also raise farmer awareness of environmental changes by providing critical information to agricultural extension officers, teachers and other supportive institutions. Researchers need to come up with innovative information on agro-ecological practices, water-saving technologies and strategies for water adaptation to climate change. This should be disseminated to ensure effective water resource management and equitable sharing among farmers to foster conflict resolution in times of water crisis.

Secondly, efficient farming strategies should be implemented within the limits of farming water costs and optimum crop water requirements under any rainfall regime to foster agricultural water productivity and profitability within farming PPFs. Yet this study has shown that farmers operating at Muooni dam site were adjusting their irrigation water without taking into consideration the depleting water resources (rainfall) and subsequent increased cost of farming water. Hence, they recorded very low water productivity and high agricultural deficits under conditions of drought. The GoK has therefore the challenge of designing policies that enhance rational water use by local stakeholders in their farming so as to narrow the gap between upstream and downstream users, present and future generations. This could be achieved if researchers devised innovative ways of merging GWS schemes with cost-effective Blue Water Supply (BWS) projects to minimise deficits in water productivity and profitability in the ASALs. Finally, implementation of such policy will require the involvement of financial and extension organisations to handle water schemes and advise on the type of participation convenient for local stakeholders. Micro-credit funds, saving schemes and insurance mutual as well as other revolving funds and banking loans will enable support for the new water schemes.

References

Ansoff, H., and E. McDonnell (1990) *Implanting Strategic Management*: New York: Prentice Hall.

Baker, M. and S. Start (1992) *Marketing and Competitive Success*. London: Philip Allen.

Breene, J. and P. Nunes (2005) "Balance, Alignment and Renewal: Understanding Competitive Essence." *Outlook* (February).

Brownlie, D., M. Saren, R. Wensley and R. Whittington (eds) (1999) *Rethinking Marketing: Towards Critical Marketing Accounting*. London: Sage.

Cateora, P. and J. Graham (1999) *International Marketing* (10th ed.) Boston: McGraw-Hill/Irwin.

CGAP-Consultative Group to Assist the Poor (2010) Good things come in small packages mobile money in Fiji. Available at: http://technology.cgap.org/2010/12/02/good-things-come-in-small-packages-mobile-money-in-fiji/

Cochoy, F. (1998) "Another Discipline for the Market Economy: Marketing as a Performative Knowledge and Know-How for Capitalism." In M. Callon (ed.) *The Laws of the Market*. Oxford: Blackwell, pp. 194–221.

Cooper, R and P. Schindler (2001) *Business Research Methods*. Boston: McGraw-Hill.

Donnelly, J.H. (1992) *Fundamentals of Management* (8th ed.). Boston: Irwin.

Doyle, P. (1992) "What are the excellent companies?" *Journal of Marketing Management* 8 (2): pp. 101–116.

Ellis, F. (1993) *Peasant Economics: Farm Households and Agrarian Development*. Cambridge: Cambridge University Press.

Ghazali, M., M. Othman, A. Yahya and M. Ibrahim (2008) "Products and Country of Origin Effects: The Malaysian Consumers' Perception."*International Review of Business Research Papers 4 (2): 91–102*.

Harris, L. and E. Ogbonna (2003) "The Organization of Marketing: A Study of Decentralized, Developed and Dispersed Marketing Activity."*Journal of Management Studies* 40 (2): 483–512.

Jaetzold, R., H. Schmidt, B. Hornetz and C. Shisanya (2007) Natural Conditions and Farm Management Information- Part C East Kenya, Subpart C1 Eastern Province."

In: Ministry of Agriculture and German Technical Cooperation (GTZ) *Farm Management Handbooks of Kenya*, Vol. II. Nairobi, pp. 1–571.

Kerlinger, F. (1986) *Foundations of Behavioural Research* (3rded.). Orlando: Harcourt Brace.

Krathwoh, D. (1998) *Methods of Educational and Social Science Research: An Integrated Approach* (2nded.). New York: Longman.

Lusch, R., S. Vargo and M. O'Brien (2007) "Competing Through Services: Insights from Service-Dominant Logic." *Journal of Retailing* 83 (1): 5–18.

Luwesi, C. (2010) *Hydro-economic Inventory in Changing Environment – An assessment of the efficiency of farming water demand under fluctuating rainfall regimes in semi-arid lands of South-East Kenya*. Saarbrücken: Lambert Academic.

Luwesi, C., C. Shisanya and J. Obando (2011) "Toward a hydro-economic approach for risk assessment and mitigation planning for farming water disasters in semi-arid Kenya." In M. Savino (ed.) *Risk Management in Environment, Production and Economy*. Rijeka: InTech, pp. 27–46.

Luwesi, C., C. Shisanya and J. Obando (2012) *Warming and Greening – The Dilemma Facing Green Water Economy under Changing Micro-Climatic Conditions in Muooni Catchment (Machakos, Kenya)*. Saarbrücken: Lambert Academic.

Luwesi, C., C. Shisanya and J. Obando (2013). Hydro-Economic Inventory Models for Planning and Evaluation of Farming Water Efficiency in a Semi-Arid Watershed of Kenya. *Journal of Agri-Food and Applied Sciences* 1 (2): 56–62

Martinsen, C. (2008) "Social marketing in sanitation: More than selling toilets."*Stockholm Water Front* (April): 14–16.

McGill, R. (2006) *Achieving Results: Performance Budgeting in the Least Developed Countries*. New York: United Nations Capital Development Fund (UNCDF).

Milles, R. and C. Snow (1978) *Organizational Strategy, Structure and Process*(5th ed.). Boston: McGraw Hill.

Mikwa J-F., C. Luwesi, R. Akombo, A. Mukashema, I. Nzeyimana, A. Ruhakana, M. Mutiso, J. Muthike and J. M. Mathenge (2014) Overlaying Spatial Parameters to Determine the Most Suitable Irrigation Strategies in Bugesera Region, Eastern Rwanda. *Journal of Agri-Food and Applied Sciences* 2(8), 242–252.

Mugenda, O. and A. Mugenda (2003) *Research methods – Quantitative and Qualitative Methods*. Nairobi: Act Press.

Ngonzo, C., C. Shisanya and J. Obando (2013) "Hydro-Geomorphologic Impact Assessment and Economic Viability of Smallholders Farms in Muooni Catchment, Machakos District."*Journal of Agri-Food and Applied Sciences* 1 (1): 16–23.

Pearce, J. and R. Robinson (2007) *Strategic Management Formulation, Implementation and Control* (10thed.) Boston: Irwin / McGraw-Hill.

Porter M. (1998) *Competitive advantage: Creating and Sustaining Superior Performance*. Springfield: Simon and Schuster.

Reichheld, F. and T. Teal (1996) *The Loyalty Effect: The Hidden Factors Behind Growth, Profits and Lasting Value*. Boston: Harvard Business School Press.

Reitbergen-McCracken, J. and H. Abaza (eds.) *Environmental Valuation: A Worldwide Compendium of Case Studies.* London: Earthscan.

Rockström, J. (2003) "Managing rain for the future." In C.M. Figueres, C. Tortajada and J. Rockström (eds) *Rethinking Water Management- Innovative Approaches to Contemporary Issues.* London: Earthscan, pp. 70–101.

Rockström, J., M. Falkenmark, L. Karlberg, H. Hoff, S. Rost, and D. Gerten (2009), "Future water availability for global food production: The potential of green water for increasing resilience to global change." Water Resources, 45, W00A12.

Wambua, P., M. Namusonge, C. Waema and C. Luwesi (2014) "Competitive strategies' effects on the market share of independent petroleum companies in Kenya." *International Journal of Innovative Research and Development* 3 (5): 149–53.

Waswa, P. (2006) "Opportunities and challenges for sustainable agricultural land management in Kenya." In P. Waswa, S. Otor and D. Mugendi (eds.) *Environment and Sustainable Development,* Vol. 1. Nairobi: Kenyatta University, pp. 52–65.

Webster, F. (2002) "The Role of Marketing and the Firm." In B. Weitz and R. Wensley (eds.) *Handbook of Marketing.* London: Sage, pp. 66–83.

Wind, Y. and T. Robertson (1983) "Marketing Strategy: New Directions for Theory and Research."*Journal of Marketing* 47 (2): 12–25.

Zeithaml, V., L. Berry and A. Pararsuraman (1990) *Delivering Quality Service: Balancing Customer Perceptions and Expectations.* New York: Free Press.

89 %

is the level of freshwater withdrawal for agriculture in Tanzania, making it the country with the highest percentage in East Africa.

5. Strengthening Formal Institutions in the Lake Victoria Basin: Role of Integrated Icts in Sustainable Irrigation Resources

Hector J. Mongi and Aloys N. Mvuma[7]

Introduction

Governance institutions in the developing world have invested a lot of their limited resources in water infrastructure to address challenges of expanding urbanisation, rapid population growth and the negative impacts of climate change. However, much of the infrastructure has fallen short of sustainability because of inadequate community participation, poor coordination and inadequate control.

One of several ways of improving participation and coordination is the use of appropriate technologies, including Information and Communication Technologies (ICTs). ICT can play a pivotal role in enabling water resource institutions to achieve the sustainability goals of Integrated Water Resource Management (IWRM). It provides tools, techniques and a common platform that allow the community to engage in giving and receiving information regarding water resources. The combination of ICT tools amplifies these advantages.

Despite this potential, the role of integrated ICT solutions in strengthening formal irrigation institutions in East Africa has not been fully analysed. This chapter seeks to identify the weaknesses of formal institutions in irrigated lands in terms of sustainable infrastructure and suggests possible integrated ICT solutions for community engagement in infrastructural projects and the coordination of water resource management. The study focuses on small-scale but sensitive irrigation schemes in Tanzania in the transboundary Lake Victoria Basin (LVB). Three districts in Mwanza Region were selected for fieldwork on the basis of three criteria: location within the transboundary LVB; the prior implementation of irrigation infrastructure projects; and the existence of formal irrigation institutions. Key informant interviews, focus group discussions and desk research were used for data collection.

Purpose

Sustainable water resources form an important topic in contemporary environmental and natural resource debates. The adoption of IWRM is generally accepted as a roadmap to sustainability. IWRM seeks to balance institutional and technological aspects in terms of economic productivity, social equity and environmental quality. However, IWRM is complex, involving many people, institutions, sectors and activities. The investment burden to support the devel-

---

7. University of Dodoma, PO Box 490, Dodoma, Tanzania. E-mail for corresponding author: hjmongi@yahoo.com

opment of large-scale water infrastructure in developing countries has largely remained with the public sector (Jägerskog and Clausen 2012; Gajigo and Lukoma 2011). This study aims to strengthen the sustainability of formal institutions in irrigated lands through ICT-supported irrigation and water resource management. The community-based water resources available for irrigation in the selected areas of LVB were corroborated; weaknesses in formal institutions at the bottom of the water-management pyramid were verified; and the roles of existing and emerging ICTs in the engagement and coordination of activities of formal institutions were identified.

Overview of Irrigation Water Resources

Agriculture is the single most water-intensive sector, especially in low- and medium-income countries. The World Bank indicates that of the 6,122m^3 of internal freshwater resources per capita worldwide, agricultural production consumes 70 % (World Bank 2014). The same source also shows that withdrawal of agricultural water is related to poverty levels. Countries classified as low income tend to withdraw the largest share of their water resources (90 %) for agriculture, while low middle, middle, upper-middle and high-income regions withdraw 88 %, 80 %, 69 % and 40 % of their water respectively. The relationship between percentage freshwater withdrawal and areas under agriculture is shown by Figure 1.

The East African region, part of sub-Saharan Africa and the low income group, has between 84 % and 90 % freshwater withdrawal for agriculture. Individual countries have varying statistics. While Tanzania leads with 89 %,

Figure 1: Regional percentages of agricultural freshwater withdrawal

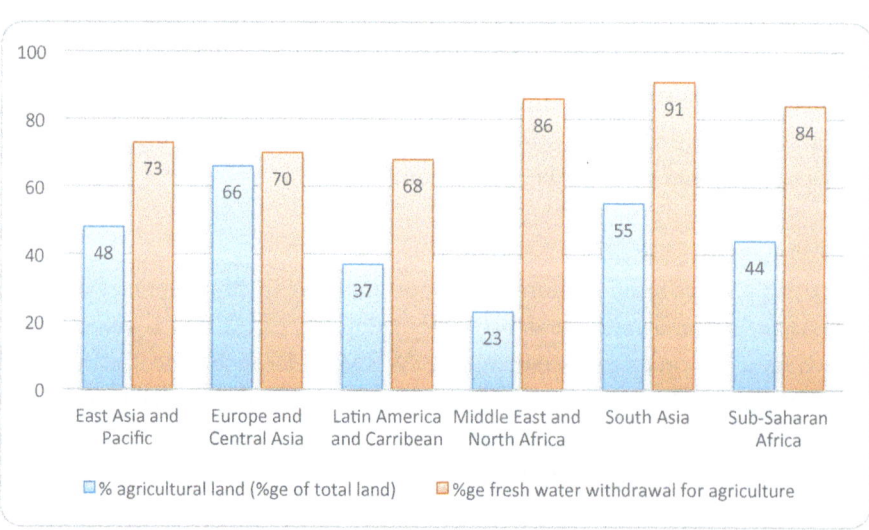

Source: World Bank (2014)

Figure 2: Country percentages for agricultural freshwater withdrawal for East Africa

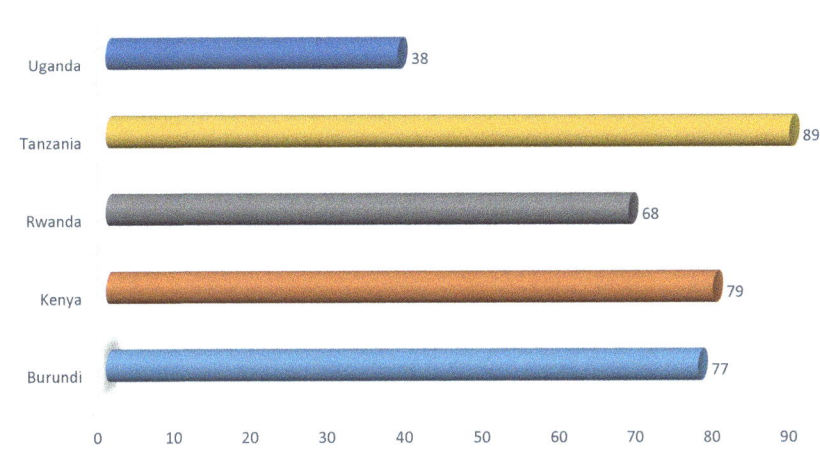

Source: World Bank (2014)

Kenya, Burundi, Rwanda and Uganda follow with 79 %, 77 %, 68 % and 38 % respectively (Figure 2).

Governments in the developing world have invested a lot of their limited resources in water infrastructure to address challenges of urbanisation, population growth and climate change. Such water resource infrastructure includes rivers, dams and other reservoirs. They form part of the irrigation infrastructure. However, the established resources have been inadequate in terms of continuous supply of water to meet the growing demands of agriculture, households and industry. In Africa, stories of less sustainable water resources are complemented by bitter statistics that show that irrigation technology has increased by 1 % in 28 years, from 3 % in 1980 to 4 % in 2008 (Gajigo and Lukoma 2011).

A survey of dams in Tanzania conducted in 2009 indicated that most of the 639 dams were in poor condition: 54 % were without crest weir; 65 % had eroded upstream slopes; 66 % had eroded downstream slopes; 55 % had eroded up/down stream slope and 53 % without riprap; 47 % of the dams had a reduced capacity; 23 % had settled embankments; 21 % were leaking; and 7 % were failed or silted up (URT 2011). Several challenges in irrigation development slow the overall attainment of food security and poverty reduction targets. According to a Tanzanian water project (URT 2007), the challenges include: poor and inappropriate irrigation infrastructure; low use of water saving and appropriate technologies; minimal use of ground water; absence of water storage structures; inadequate investment in irrigation; climate change and variability; and weak institutions responsible for irrigation management. Weak formal institutions have been associated with the under-performance or failure of irrigation schemes in developing countries, leading to the loss of expensive resource investments.

Irrigation is considered an option in combating the social and environmental challenges facing food production. The National Irrigation Master Plan (NIMP) revealed that the irrigation potential in Tanzania is 29.4 million hectares. Although much of it (22.3 million hectares) is classified as low potential, a significant area is classified as high (2.3 million hectares) and medium potential (4.8 million hectares) (URT 2002a). Tanzania is setting higher targets for irrigation. For example, it is expected that by 2020, the land under irrigation will increase from the current 400,000 hectares to 2 million hectares, a fivefold increase. Such ambitious targets require more water infrastructure as well as strengthened institutions in irrigation schemes. Droogers and Bastiaanssen (2009) conducted an evaluation of five irrigation schemes in the Tanzania part of LVB. LVB is a transboundary ecosystem shared among five countries: Burundi, Kenya, Rwanda, Tanzania and Uganda. It has numerous water resources, which are key to its potential for irrigated agriculture. The evaluated irrigation schemes were Mara Valley, Bugwema, Isanga, Manonga and Ngono. Most are at various stages of development. Institutional support for these schemes was generally ranked highly. However, as they develop, there is a greater need for establishing and strengthening formal institutions to ensure sustainable irrigation-resource management.

Formal Institutions in Irrigation Water Resource Management in Tanzania

The Tanzanian irrigation policy of 2009 lists the formal institutions by category: National, Zonal, Local Government and Community levels (Table 1).

The National Water Policy (NAWAPO) 2002 requires the establishment of an organisational structure that is simple, transparent, efficient and accountable to community needs. Tanzanian irrigation institutions have not been devoid of weaknesses. Despite many institutional reforms, poor coordination is the single most significant weakness. Others are conflicting objectives and roles in irriga-

Table 1: Irrigation institutions by levels

Level	Institutions
National (Central Govt)	Ministries responsible for water, irrigation, national-based NGOs
Zonal (Central Govt)	River basins management, zonal irrigation offices, zonal-based NGOs and zonal-based private sector
Local Government	District irrigation offices, district-based NGOs, Community-based organizations CBOs and private sector
Communities	Irrigation organisations, farmers/irrigators, CBOs

Source: URT (2002a)

Table 2: General institutional roles by levels

Level	Roles
National and Zonal	Coordination of sectoral stakeholders Establishment and enforcement of irrigation regulations Timely financing, provision of equipment and facilities Strengthen irrigation data-collection Capacitate institutions through training
Local Government	Identification of irrigation schemes Planning and designing Construction Operation and maintenance of irrigation schemes
Communities	Participate in scheme development/ improvement Collection and management of irrigation service charges Operation and maintenance of irrigation infrastructure Establish irrigation database and link up with national database Coordinate support to irrigators and organisations in irrigation interventions

Sources: URT (2002b)

tion infrastructure management, inadequate enforcement of laws and regulations as well as corruption and inadequate accountability, lack of transparency and participation by stakeholders. The specific roles of each level as listed in the national irrigation master plan (URT 2002a) are shown in Table 2.

Weaknesses in Formal Institutions Managing Irrigation Water Resources in Tanzania
The Tanzania irrigation policy of 2009 lists types of formal institutional weakness by National, Zonal, Local Government and Community levels (Table 3). However, due to the varying socioeconomic development of the country, study-

Table 3: General institutional weaknesses by levels

Level	Weaknesses
National and Zonal	Poor institutional setup Lack of irrigation regulations Inadequate qualified staff Inadequate financing Inadequate equipment and facilities
Local Government	Inadequate database Lack of awareness of roles and responsibilities Inadequate skills and financing Weak enforcement of by-laws Inadequate equipment and facilities
Communities	Limited funds Limited capacity in financial management Weak leadership Limited capacity to enforce laws Limited capacity to ensure sustainability of infrastructure

Sources: URT (2002a)

ing a specific area allows for verification of the weaknesses mentioned and possible identification of further weaknesses.

Integrated ICTs for Water Resource Management

One of several ways of strengthening the formal institutions of irrigation schemes is the use of appropriate technologies, including ICT. ICT refers to technologies that manipulate and communicate information. They include storage devices such as magnetic disk/tape, optical disks (CD/DVD) and flash memory; broadcasting technology such as radio and television; data and information processing technology like computers; and voice, sound and image technologies such as microphone, camera, loudspeaker, telephone to cellular phones; and technology for automated wireless data capture and transmission.

The role of ICTs in supporting decision-making, coordination and control of water resources is uncontested. Mobile and fixed phones, radios, the Internet and other emerging technologies are capable of enhancing decision-making through participation and information-sharing (Hellström 2010; Karanasios 2011; Ospina and Heeks 2010; Duncombe and Boateng 2009). They can also enhance control through informed policy making and enforcement of laws and regulations related to water resources. Sife et al. (2007) argue that ICTs can improve information accessibility; facilitate communication via electronic facilities; enhancing synchronous learning; and increase cooperation and collaboration. Therefore, apart from being coordination tools, ICTs can also be useful capacity-building tools for strengthening institutions in irrigation schemes.

Between 2010 and 2014, researchers at the University of Dodoma in Tanzania (including the authors) led a collaborative project to develop integrated ICTs for water resource governance in the LVB.

The situational analysis and needs-assessment parts of the project involved stakeholders from all water-related sectors such as agriculture, industry, households, policy and environment at various scales, from micro, meso to macro. The main research output was Water Resource Governance System (WaGoSy), an integrated ICT solution for addressing governance challenges relating to LVB water resources (Mvuma et al. 2014). The system comprises the following components or modules: Web-Based Portal (WaGoSy-WBP), Water Quality Reporter (WaGoSy-WQR), Wireless Sensor Network (WaGoSy-WSN), Open Meeting (WaGoSy-OM), Visualisation (WaGoSy-V) and SMS Box (WaGoSY-SMSB) (see Figure 3).

WaGoSy-WBP comprises Wiki, RSS Newsfeed, Commenting and Posting services. The module provides an ideal platform for fast information creation, dissemination and sharing to create awareness, facilitate participation and enhance transparency.

WaGoSy-WQR is an Arduino-based water quality sensing platform that uses

Figure 3: Overall architecture of the Water Resource Governance System

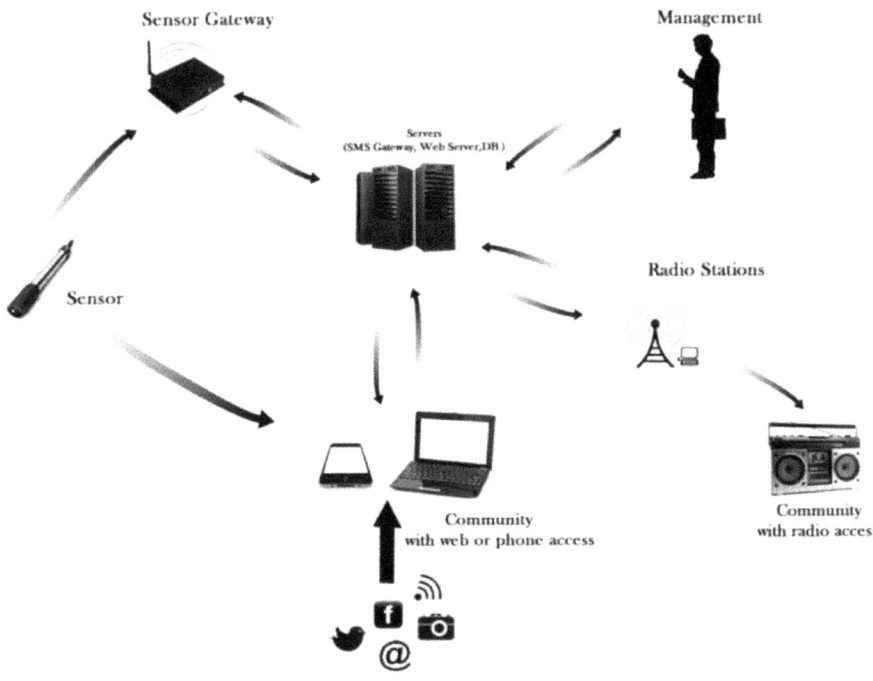

Source: Faustine et al. (2014)

a smartphone application based on Android programming. It enables local water quality agents to capture and send water quality parameters to the central database and receive quality status notifications via SMS. It consists of sensors for pH, electrical conductivity, dissolved oxygen and temperature and requires an Android smartphone OS Version 2.3.x. The module supports participation by the local community in water quality monitoring. It also enhances awareness among stakeholders on water quality. Furthermore, it improves accountability and transparency.

WaGoSy-WSN is a network of sensor nodes that enables automatic and continuous capturing of water quality parameters from a site and submits them to the central database (Faustine et al. 2014). It consists of WSN nodes with sensors and a WSN gateway. Each WSN node is equipped with four basic sensors that provide a general characterisation of water quality and a GPS for capturing geospatial parameters. WSN nodes and gateway use an XBee-Pro module operating in the ZigBee mode, which uses a 2.4 GHz unlicensed band and consumes very little power (Faustine and Aloys 2012). Both modules are implemented using an Arduino microcontroller, an open source electronics prototyping platform. The gateway is equipped with a solar panel to provide continuous power.

The WaGoSy-OM module was developed using Java technology. It enables water resource stakeholders to communicate in real time through text, audio and video.

The WaGoSy-V module was developed using Hypertext Mark-up Language (HTML) and Java Scripts. It enables stakeholders to visualise and map water quality parameters and locations graphically from the WaGoSy-WQR and WaGoSy-WSN modules. From the graphs, users can observe the behaviour of each parameter and alert the public in case of abnormality. The module is of great use in monitoring and controlling water resources. It also assists in informed decision-making, enhances enforcement of laws and regulations and improves accountability and transparency.

The WaGoSy-SMSB module is a compact, low-cost solution for sending and receiving Short Message Service (SMS) messages using a common Subscriber Identury Module (SIM) card. It includes a Global System for Mobile Communications (GSM) quad-band modem and a micro Secure Digital (SD) memory card to store messages. It also has a Debian Unix system to manage the SMS and Multimedia Message Service (MMS) queues through an easy-to-use Web interface integrated into the main system. The general community can report events related to water resources such as catchment fire, water use conflicts, illegal fishing, water pollution and illegal farming near water catchment areas. This module enables local radio presenters to directly interact with the community by viewing and reading SMSs sent by the community from the computer or phone browser. It also relays classified SMSs to classified actors for appropriate actions. Message broadcasting and alerting is also supported by this module.

Research Questions

The study sought to answer the following questions:
i. Which water resources were confirmed by the community to be available for irrigation in the selected areas of LVB?
ii. To what extent did the stated weaknesses of formal institutions match the reality at the bottom of the irrigation management pyramid in the selected areas of LVB?
iii. What roles could the existing and emerging ICTs play in engaging and co-ordinating the activities of formal institutions in LVB?

Methodology

The study was conducted in Mwanza Region, Tanzania, one of the potential areas within LVB. Three districts, Ilemela, Nyamagana and Kwimba, were selected in the region. Selection criteria included the presence of formal irrigation schemes, potential knowledge and use of ICT tools and potential community support in providing information. In each district, the following formal institutions were selected for detailed study: Umoja wa Wakulima Maiga (UWAMA)

Figure 3: Research sites in Mwanza, Tanzania

Source: Field data, 2014

– *Association of Paddy Farmers in Maiga* – from Kwimba District; Igembensabo Irrigation Group (IIG), Ilemela; and Umoja wa Wakulima Bustani (UWABU) – *Gardeners' Association*, Nyamagana.

UWAMA is an irrigator association made up of 13 irrigation groups. It performs its activities within the Maiga Irrigation Scheme (MIS), which started in 1996 with a small weir as infrastructure. However, the weir could not meet increasing demand, thus overuse of water to meet crop production, livestock keeping and domestic needs led to its collapse in 2000. UWAMA is made up of 186 members, of which 97 are male and 89 female. There are 22 other groups in varying stages of formalisation as irrigator associations. The National Irrigation Development Fund (NIDF) has supported capacity-building to enable formalisation of the irrigation association. The main capacity-building issues are constitutions, registration and linkage with financial institutions. IIG and UWABU are small-scale irrigator groups that have also received much support for irrigation infrastructure. However, consistent with a general trend, such infrastructure, including irrigation equipment and water resources, has not been sustainable.

The study adopted a qualitative research paradigm. Data were mainly collected through discussions with members of irrigation associations, with key

Table 4: Participants in open space discussions by category, district and gender

Category	District						Total
	Ilemela		Nyamagana		Kwimba		
	Male	Female	Male	Female	Male	Female	
Farmers	19	3	9	18	19	8	76
Leaders	4	2	5	0	0	0	11
Experts	1	4	0	0	5	0	10
Sub-total	24	9	14	18	24	8	
Grand total	33		32		32		97

Source: Field data, 2014

informants, and by reviewing the relevant literature. The membership composition of the formal irrigation institutions in each district is shown in Table 4.

Discussions were held in two rounds using different methods. First, the open space method was adopted, whereby all participants joined in a plenary to corroborate the weaknesses of their formal institutions.

Second, there were discussions in two small focus groups of between 14 and 16 participants. These discussions were held in each district to gain an insight into each of the identified weaknesses. The discussions led to the regrouping of the weaknesses, so that related factors were grouped together. Secondary data, including a literature review, were used to enrich the results and discussions on how an appropriate combination of ICTs in the WaGoSy system could address the challenges facing formal institutions in irrigation schemes. Data collected were analysed using both qualitative and quantitative methods. Content analysis helped in grouping related items on institutional weaknesses, while qualitative data were summarised in frequency tables. Graphical data are presented and described accordingly.

Figure 4: Participants after discussion sessions in Kwimba District in Mwanza Tanzania

Source: Field data, 2014

Results and Discussions

Community-based Water Resources in the Study Area

Presence of water resources is key to irrigation activities. The type of water resources available determines the irrigation infrastructure to be developed. The first objective of this study was to understand the type of community-based water resources.

Table 5: Perceived water resources by district in the study area

SN	Water resource	District		
		Ilemela	Nyamagana	Kwimba
1	Deep wells	✓	✓	x
2	Shallow wells	✓	✓	✓
3	Charcoal dams	✓	✓	x
4	Seasonal streams	✓	✓	✓
5	Seasonal rivers	x	✓	✓
6	Permanent rivers	x	x	x
7	Dams	x	x	✓
8	Lake	x	x	x

Source: Field data, 2014

Lake Victoria is the largest freshwater body in Africa and the second largest in the world – second to Lake Superior in North America (Anon 1998; Akumu et al. 2010). It is a few kilometres from the study sites in Ilemela and Nyamagana. However, despite its potential, it was not mentioned among the water resources for irrigation in the communities. Participants in the research only valued the resources that have a direct impact on their activities. For the lake to have a positive impact on irrigation, appropriate infrastructure is required that not only serves the communities nearby but also does not contribute to more national and international conflict.

Corroborated Weaknesses of Formal Institutions in the Study Area

The general weaknesses of formal institutions at various levels are well documented (see Table 3). However, they are not corroborated at specific locations with varying socioeconomic and biophysical conditions. A first step in addressing a problem is to understand its depth – including its root cause. Participants in this study identified a cluster of five problems and their causes. The clusters are fragmentation, centralisation, awareness, accountability and finances (Figure 5). This cluster presents a slightly different version from the general one, with key problems unique to the typical irrigation institutions at the base of pyramid.

Fragmentation of institutional elements: Water resource management has a multi-sector aspect. Although this study focuses on the lowest level of the institutional framework, the problem of fragmentation of policy and decision-making was

Figure 5: Formal institutional weaknesses identified in selected irrigation areas in Mwanza

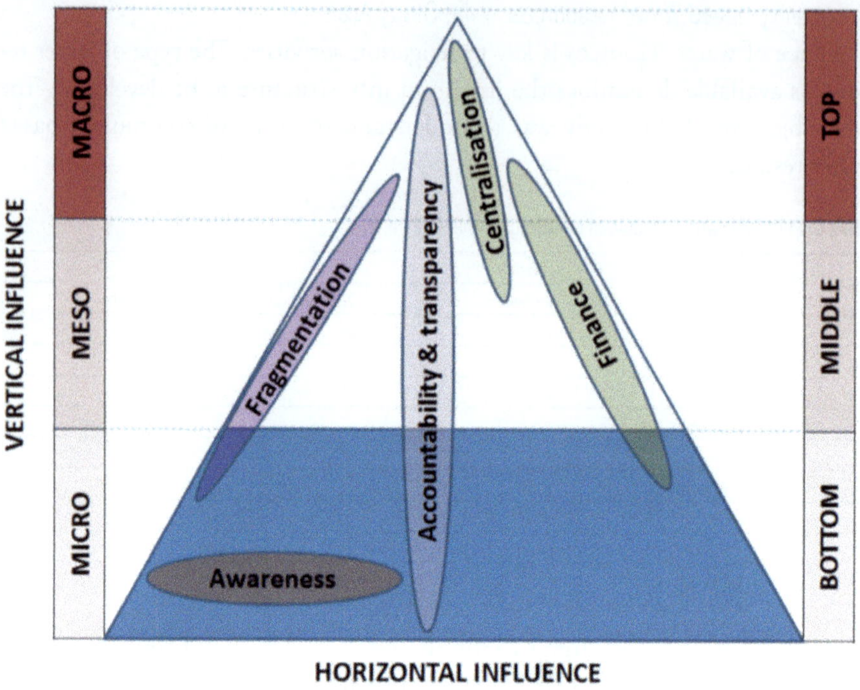

Source: Field data, 2014

highlighted across scales (Figure 5). Agriculture (thus irrigation), livestock and water for domestic use were addressed by different ministries at macro and meso scales. At the very bottom level, fragmentation was expressed in terms of inequitable distribution of irrigation equipment and access to infrastructure. Equity issues are central to fragmentation, which eventually affect all other parameters such as training, income and gender. This was partly the reason for failure of irrigation infrastructure projects and eventually the weakening of irrigation institutions in Ilemela and Nyamagana Districts. In Kwimba District, the story was slightly different, but with similar sustainability challenges. Fragmentation is related to multiple users. For example, Maiga Dam was designed for multiple uses: livestock, crop irrigation, fishery, as well as domestic. However, across all districts and even beyond, high demand for irrigation water versus supply has been a common source of conflict between livestock keepers and crop producers. Involvement of stakeholders and enhancing ownership of the resource among competing interests could lessen conflicts and strengthen the institutions mandated to manage the resources.

Centralisation of decision making and implementation: Inadequate community involvement in issues related to irrigation water as well as infrastructural project implementation was considered a weakness in formal institutions in the study

Figure 6: Chairperson of UWABU in Nyamagana District explaining the failure of water pumps and a deep well project

Source: Field data, 2014

areas. The central government (macro scale) and some local government institutions (meso scale) tended to make decisions and implement projects on behalf of the community (micro scale) (see Figure 5). This not only led to lengthy decision-making process, but also did not enhance ownership of infrastructure at the lowest level. Lack of ownership by the community of users is demonstrated by the collapse of Kwimba weir. In Nyamagana, new water pumps and shallow well projects were not sustainable partly due to inadequate community involvement (Figure 6). There was limited maintenance of and security for the infrastructure.

Insufficient awareness: Members of the formal irrigation schemes admitted their low involvement in policy-making, as well as in formulating rules and regulations they are supposed to follow. Policy, rules and regulations are among the five pillars of IWRM (ECOWAS, 2006) and therefore a source of strength of formal institutions. For instance, inadequate awareness of (something is missing here), water use conflicts and inadequate participation in infrastructural development were perceived critical hindrances to sustainability. Lack of awareness and illiteracy were also perceived as precursor of the irresponsibility among members in meeting their membership obligations. The challenge lies in increasing civil society capacity and its scope to use the political and public space to engage with and influence government decision-making and democratic practice.

Low levels of accountability and transparency: Accountability and transparency are important pillars in governance and cut across scales (see Figure 5). The two pillars were expressed in terms of budgetary reporting (revenues and expenditures) and disbursement procedures. Participants expressed willingness to pay for water use, and contribute to infrastructural maintenance and operations as well as conservation measures if all proceedings were transparent and leaders demonstrated high standards of accountability.

Inadequate access to finances: The financial resources to implement and support the activities of micro-scale formal institutions were limited, even though these institutions have roles in the planning, design, implementation and maintenance of water resource infrastructure. One reason for this underfunding was inadequate financial management capacity and tools for mobilising financial resources within and outside the community. The problem of inadequate funding cut across the institutional framework, but was felt at the bottom of the scale.

Strengthening Formal Institutions in LVB through Integrated ICTs

ICT, and specifically WaGoSy, provides tools that can address most of the institutional challenges mentioned above (see Figure 3). The weaknesses of formal institutions in the study area in terms of equitability, environmental quality and sustainability, can be summarised as fragmentation, duplication, centralisation and lack of sustainability. WaGoSy, though targeting multi-scale solutions to water resource governance, can contribute to strengthening these institutions in the following ways:

Defragmentation and multi-scale coordination of institutional issues: WaGoSy is an integrated system with a number of options for engaging communities in the collective performance of formal institutions in irrigation schemes. It provides one-stop ICT-based solutions for improved coordination between institutional management units. Apart from providing citizens with data and information sharing, WaGoSy could empower members of formal institutions to demand better services from their leaders at the bottom, as well as at the meso and micro levels. The concept behind the design and development of WaGoSy in engaging multi-scale stakeholders is similar to the way an architect designs a multi-storey building to replace isolated huts. In this analogy, hut occupants, who could not meet easily, would be able to interact and share information through common venues like lounges, restaurants and even corridors. The WaGoSy components are these venues.

The collection of servers making WaGoSy (Web server, Database and SMS gateway) is a convergence and divergence point. Data and information collected from across the institutional framework of water resource management, including water for irrigation, are stored, manipulated and shared. WaGoSy is capable of sending the same data or information to key stakeholders depending on their roles in water resource management. These may include policy-makers, law enforcers, decision-makers and members of formal water resource institutions at various scales.

WaGoSy-WBP is a door to social media tools such as Facebook, LinkedIn and Twitter where more citizens, especially youths, can create networks among themselves as well as with government. It is a mechanism for linking the public to their government in managing water resources. According to Pera (Mvuma 2014), social media can improve interactivity between government and public, allowing officials in government to build relationships with the citizens they represent. They can enhance government abilities to interact with citizens and transform the way organisations can communicate with the public.

Cost-effective awareness building at the bottom level: Awareness is often linked to democracy. Citizens' awareness of their rights is a precursor to strong participation in the activities of formal water institutions in irrigated lands. WaGoSy offers solutions that can enhance participation by a greater proportion of institutional members in irrigation schemes. Integration of radio and mobile phones, two devices that have been spreading rapidly, can substantially contribute to awarenessbuilding at the bottom of pyramid. The system provides both horizontal and vertical opportunities to network among institutions and their members. WaGoSy-OM and WaGoSy-SMSB are considered cost-effective means of getting people to meet and share information and knowledge through virtual environments. Although access to the Internet to support online meetings is still

Figure 7: Radio is an important mass media tool among livestock keepers in the LVB. WaGoSy via community radios can bridge the digital divide created by multiple communication networks

Source: Field data, 2014

a problem, especially in rural areas where most irrigation schemes are located, the recent proliferation of high-end mobile phones associated with the increased investment in mobile networks; provide the opportunity for critical mass participation through social media.

Improving accountability and transparency: Reporting to and report dissemination among water resource stakeholders are techniques for enhancing transparency and accountability. WaGoSy is an integrated system with a number of options for engaging communities in the collective performance of irrigation management activities.

WaGoSy-WBP is also integrated with a Geographic Information System (GIS), which helps to locate sensors and their respective data-points. In the network of sensors, each node represents a data-point for the most pressing issues in water management in relation to irrigation, fishing, livestock, as well as domestic utilities. GIS can report the location data of the sensors in geospatial form (i.e., latitudes and longitudes) with associated attributes (e.g., name of the location). Data can therefore be collected in quantitative forms like pH, dissolved oxygen, water temperatures and conductivity with location data for quick action on variations beyond certain configured thresholds or for monitoring purposes. For example, WaGoSy has intelligent capability that can send automated alerts in the form of SMSs and/or e-mails wherever a pre-established pH threshold of 7.2 is exceeded. Such alerts originate from data collected through WaGoSy-WQR and WaGoSy-WSN and analysed through WaGoSy-V and are sent to selected individuals or groups depending on their responsibilities in water management. The two system components are tools to reliably trace critical points of water pollution by reporting to the relevant responsible persons: law enforcers, institution leaders or to other scales within water management. Qualitative data collected via community-based crowd-sourcing such as text messages, photo images and short videos can also be geo-tagged to locate the place where they were collected. Apart from informing the community about the state of their water resources and surrounding environment, such data can also be used in planning, maintenance, monitoring and evaluation. WaGoSy, through these capabilities, provides a platform for learning and capacity building. Short messages, photo images and short videos can be shared through a web-based portal, by radio (where reflections about the information can be shared) as well as through mobile phones.

Mobilising and managing financial resources: ICT promotes e-engagement in the processes of policy decision-making. Apart from text messages and information-sharing by radios, the use of social media as provided by WaGoSy can develop trust; enhance transparency through information interactions; as well as build an online network (Lee and Kim 2014).

Figure 8: Voluntary labourer constructing an irrigation canal in Kwimba District. High standards of accountability and transparency are the motivation for this kind of participation

Source: Field data, 2014

One of several ways in which ICT redundancy can contribute to water governance is by improved access to financial capital. Mobile phones and radios are the most important ICTs available for the bottom level of water management institutions. Situation analysis done for the design of WaGoSy indicated that on average 29.8 % and 30.4 % owned radios and mobile handsets respectively (Mvuma 2014). However, accessibility data are much higher due, for instance, to owning a SIM card without a phone or owning multiple SIM cards and subscribing to more than one mobile network provider. WaGoSy is an integrated system with a number of options for engaging communities in the collective performance of irrigation management activities. Redundancy in the context of ICT refers to the potential of these tools to increase the availability of resources (Ospina and Heeks 2010). Application of this situation to the water sector may be through access to capital for efficient water use facilities, improved systems of water distribution, and also access to markets linked to water use efficiency. In the agricultural sector, mobile phones and Internet usage among Tanzania's small farmers were found to increase their participation in markets and to provide information on improved productivity (SIDA 2009). Excess income from the agricultural sector may allow for re-investment in water for agriculture by acquiring efficient irrigation facilities and engaging in conservation on water sources.

Conclusions and Suggestion for Future Studies

Formal institutions in irrigation schemes continue to face challenges in managing water resources as a result of competing needs. There are general weaknesses identified at national, local and community scales. However, at a very specific community scale and in relation to specific water users, the challenges are slightly different. This study involved the community in identifying those weaknesses and it suggests combined ICT tools to address them. The focus was on WaGoSy, a system developed to address governance challenges and with practical application in strengthening institutions that are managing water resources at micro levels. Formal institutions with demands for training need databases that are linked to top institutions, and need to be aware of their roles and responsibilities as well as capacity to coordinate both horizontally and vertically. The use of relevant integrated ICT solutions will help to align the activities with goals and thereby strengthen the institutions. WaGoSy is still at a pilot stage and requires evaluation. Further studies should focus on the extent to which integrated ICTs engage formal institutions' members in achieving sustainable goals for water for irrigation. This could be preceded by a relevance evaluation framework to serve as the foundation for the study.

Key Policy and Research Implications

The policies and strategies within the East African Community (EAC) underscore the importance of freshwater resources to all key sectors of the economy. Demand for fresh water at Global and regional scale is increasing amid declining supplies for agriculture, industry and households. Agriculture is the most intensive user of freshwater resources through irrigation. EAC's Agriculture and Rural Development Policy of 2006 emphasises two major challenges in improving irrigation: (i) limited appropriate technological development and (ii) inadequate resources to manage and develop utilisation of water resources. One of the policies for increased agricultural production and productivity is the promotion of community participation in the development of irrigation, water management and the maintenance of irrigation infrastructure. Tanzania's Water Policy of 2002 identifies the key challenges hindering sustainable water management, including dry spells and droughts, water scarcity and conflicts, lack of information on water quality and quantity as well as inadequate coordination of cross-sectoral issues. Strong management institutions are needed for agricultural water resources at various scales from micro and meso to macro.

ICT is one of the appropriate technologies to support these institutions. These tools enhance pre- and post-development of irrigation infrastructures. They can enhance, in horizontal fashion, member participation in the institutions that plan, designate, construct and maintain infrastructures. They can also support coordination of cross-sectoral issues by linking stakeholders in both vertical and horizontal fashion. ICT options have been used in the region to support community participation, accountability and transparency. Specific examples are the integrated ICT solutions for the governance of water resources in the LVB that were developed under the VicRes Programme of the Inter-University Council of East Africa (IUCEA) with financial support from the Swedish International Development Agency (SIDA). The project was in response to the evaluation in the third EAC strategic plan (2006–10), which emphasised the importance of knowledge and communications in fast-tracking the development agenda. This ambitious strategy of making LVB a hub of information-sharing was not achieved.

Apart from contributing policy insights into enhanced irrigation by tackling before-and-after infrastructure development issues in community-based projects, this chapter also highlights the important research and development implications of integrated ICTs. While water institutions are charged with conducting research in collaboration with partners, such research has not been effective due to inadequate coordination and low budgets. ICTs can improve research coordination and make available data that are collected by semi-automatic or fully automatic tools, or which are crowd-sourced through community participation.

Acknowledgements

The authors wish to thank the LVB communities for their participation in the study; SIDA through the IUCEA and German Academic Exchange Services (DAAD) for financial resources; and the Nordic African Institute (NAI) for supporting the dissemination of the findings in a variety of ways.

References

Akumu, J., G. Bwanuka, I. Makombe and I. Chamwali (2010) "Improving Livelihoods of Fishing Communities in the Lake Victoria Basin: An Overview of Selected Landing Sites in Uganda." In R. Mdegela, J. Rutaisire, J. Obua and S. Okoth (eds) Fisheries and Aquaculture Proceedings of the Cluster Workshop, 12-14 December 2010, Mwanza, Tanzania, pp 7–20, http://www.cabdirect.org/abstracts/20133300817.html

Anon (1998) Think Quest. The living Africa: The Land-lake Victoria. Online Resource at Library.thinkquest.org

Droogers, P. and W. Bastiaanssen (2009) Irrigation Potential Lake Victoria, Tanzania: Mara Valley, Bugwema, Isanga, Manonga and Ngono, WaterWatch /Nile Basin Initiative, http://www.futurewater.nl/downloads/2008_Droogers_NBI.pdf

Duncombe, R. and R. Boateng (2009) "Mobile Phones and Financial Services in Developing Countries: a review of concepts, methods, issues, evidence and future research directions." *Third World Quarterly* 30(7): 1237–58.

ECOWAS (2006) Integrated Water Resource Management, Economic Community of West African States, www.ecowas.int

Faustine, A., A. Mvuma, H. Mongi, M. Gabriel, A. Tenge and S. Kucel (2014) Wireless Sensor Networks for Water Quality Monitoring and Control within Lake Victoria Basin: Prototype Development, Wireless Sensor Network, 2014, 6, 281–290, http://www.scirp.org/Journal/PaperDownload.aspx?paperID=52250

Faustine, A. and A. Mvuma (2012) "Design and Simulation of Wireless Sensor Network for Water Quality Monitoring around Lake Victoria." *Journal of Informatics and Virtual Education* 2(1), pp 37–42.

Gajigo, O. and A. Lukoma (2011) "Infrastructure and Agricultural Productivity in Africa" African Development Bank Marketing Brief.

Hellström, J. (2010) "The Innovative Use of Mobile Applications in East Africa." *Sida Review*, December 2010.

Jägerskog, A. and T. Clausen (eds) (2012) Feeding a Thirsty World – Challenges and Opportunities for a Water and Food Secure Future. Report No. 31. Stockholm International Water Institute (SIWI), Stockholm. Available at http://www.worldwaterweek.org/documents/Resources/Reports/Feeding_a_thirsty_world_2012worldwaterweek_report_31

Karanasios, S. (2011) New and Emerging ICTs and Climate Change in Developing Countries. Centre for Development Informatics, Institute for Development Policy and Management, University of Manchester.

Lee, J. and S. Kim (2014) "Active Citizen E-Participation in Local Governance: Do IndividualSocial Capital and E-Participation Management Matter?" Proceedings of the 47th Annual HICSS conference, Hawaii, pp. 2044–2053.

Mvuma, A., A. Tenge, S. Kucel, H. Mongi and M. Gabriel (2014) ICT and Adaptation to Climate Change: Innovative and integrated solutions to address challenges of water resource governance within Lake Victoria Basin. Final Report, VicRes/Inter-University Council for East Africa (IUCEA).

Ospina, A. and R. Heeks (2010) *Unveiling the Links between ICTs and Climate Change in Developing Countries: A Scoping Study.* Ottawa: International Development Research Centre.

Pera, A. (2014) "The Use of Educational Psychology to Explain Economic Behavior." *Economics, Management, and Financial Markets* 9(1): 112–17.

SIDA (2009) Information and Communication Technologies for the Enhancement of Democracy – with a Focus on Empowerment. Available at www.Sida.se/publications

Sife, A., E. Lwoga and C. Sanga (2007) "New technologies for teaching and learning: Challenges for higher learning institutions in developing countries." *International Journal of Education and Development using ICT* 3(2): 57–67.

URT (United Republic of Tanzania) (2002a) National Irrigation Master Plan. Dar es Salaam: Ministry of Agriculture, Food Security and Cooperatives/Japanese International Development Agency.

URT (2002b) National Water Policy. Dar es Salaam: Ministry of Water.

URT (2007) Water Sector Development Project. Dar es Salaam: Ministry of Water.

URT (2011) Water Sector Status Report 2011: With a Summary of Water Sector Progress since 2007. Dar es salaam: Ministry of Water.

World Bank (2014) *The Little Green Data Book*. Washington DC: International Bank for Reconstruction and Development/ World Bank.

CURRENT AFRICAN ISSUES PUBLISHED BY THE INSTITUTE

Recent issues in the series are available electronically
for download free of charge www.nai.uu.se

1981
1. *South Africa, the West and the Frontline States. Report from a Seminar.*
2. Maja Naur, *Social and Organisational Change in Libya.*
3. *Peasants and Agricultural Production in Africa. A Nordic Research Seminar. Follow-up Reports and Discussions.*

1985
4. Ray Bush & S. Kibble, *Destabilisation in Southern Africa, an Overview.*
5. Bertil Egerö, *Mozambique and the Southern African Struggle for Liberation.*

1986
6. Carol B.Thompson, *Regional Economic Polic under Crisis Condition. Southern African Development.*

1989
7. Inge Tvedten, *The War in Angola, Internal Conditions for Peace and Recovery.*
8. Patrick Wilmot, *Nigeria's Southern Africa Policy 1960–1988.*

1990
9. Jonathan Baker, *Perestroika for Ethiopia: In Search of the End of the Rainbow?*
10. Horace Campbell, *The Siege of Cuito Cuanavale.*

1991
11. Maria Bongartz, *The Civil War in Somalia. Its genesis and dynamics.*
12. Shadrack B.O. Gutto, *Human and People's Rights in Africa. Myths, Realities and Prospects.*
13. Said Chikhi, *Algeria. From Mass Rebellion to Workers' Protest.*
14. Bertil Odén, *Namibia's Economic Links to South Africa.*

1992
15. Cervenka Zdenek, *African National Congress Meets Eastern Europe. A Dialogue on Common Experiences.*

1993
16. Diallo Garba, *Mauritania–The Other Apartheid?*

1994
17. Zdenek Cervenka and Colin Legum, *Can National Dialogue Break the Power of Terror in Burundi?*
18. Erik Nordberg and Uno Winblad, *Urban Environmental Health and Hygiene in Sub-Saharan Africa.*

1996
19. Chris Dunton and Mai Palmberg, *Human Rights and Homosexuality in Southern Africa.*

1998
20. Georges Nzongola-Ntalaja, *From Zaire to the Democratic Republic of the Congo.*

1999
21. Filip Reyntjens, *Talking or Fighting? Political Evolution in Rwanda and Burundi, 1998–1999.*
22. Herbert Weiss, *War and Peace in the Democratic Republic of the Congo.*

2000
23. Filip Reyntjens, *Small States in an Unstable Region – Rwanda and Burundi, 1999–2000.*

2001
24. Filip Reyntjens, *Again at the Crossroads: Rwanda and Burundi, 2000–2001.*
25. Henning Melber, *The New African Initiative and the African Union. A Preliminary Assessment and Documentation.*

2003
26. Dahilon Yassin Mohamoda, *Nile Basin Cooperation. A Review of the Literature.*

2004
27. Henning Melber (ed.), *Media, Public Discourse and Political Contestation in Zimbabwe.*

28. Georges Nzongola-Ntalaja, *From Zaire to the Democratic Republic of the Congo.* (Second and Revised Edition)

2005

29. Henning Melber (ed.), *Trade, Development, Cooperation – What Future for Africa?*
30. Kaniye S.A. Ebeku, *The Succession of Faure Gnassingbe to the Togolese Presidency – An International Law Perspective.*
31. J.V. Lazarus, C. Christiansen, L. Rosendal Østergaard, L.A. Richey, *Models for Life – Advancing antiretroviral therapy in sub-Saharan Africa.*

2006

32. Charles Manga Fombad & Zein Kebonang, *AU, NEPAD and the APRM – Democratisation Efforts Explored.* (Ed. H. Melber.)
33. P.P. Leite, C. Olsson, M. Schöldtz, T. Shelley, P. Wrange, H. Corell and K. Scheele, *The Western Sahara Conflict – The Role of Natural Resources in Decolonization.* (Ed. Claes Olsson)

2007

34. Jassey, Katja and Stella Nyanzi, *How to Be a "Proper" Woman in the Times of HIV and AIDS.*
35. M. Lee, H. Melber, S. Naidu and I. Taylor, *China in Africa.* (Compiled by Henning Melber)
36. Nathaniel King, *Conflict as Integration. Youth Aspiration to Personhood in the Teleology of Sierra Leone's 'Senseless War'.*

2008

37. Aderanti Adepoju, *Migration in sub-Saharan Africa.*
38. Bo Malmberg, *Demography and the development potential of sub-Saharan Africa.*
39. Johan Holmberg, *Natural resources in sub-Saharan Africa: Assets and vulnerabilities.*
40. Arne Bigsten and Dick Durevall, *The African economy and its role in the world economy.*

41. Fantu Cheru, *Africa's development in the 21st century: Reshaping the research agenda.*

2009

42. Dan Kuwali, *Persuasive Prevention. Towards a Principle for Implementing Article 4(h) and R2P by the African Union.*
43. Daniel Volman, *China, India, Russia and the United States. The Scramble for African Oil and the Militarization of the Continent.*

2010

44. Mats Hårsmar, *Understanding Poverty in Africa? A Navigation through Disputed Concepts, Data and Terrains.*

2011

45. Sam Maghimbi, Razack B. Lokina and Mathew A. Senga, *The Agrarian Question in Tanzania? A State of the Art Paper.*
46. William Minter, *African Migration, Global Inequalities, and Human Rights. Connecting the Dots.*
47. Musa Abutudu and Dauda Garuba, *Natural Resource Governance and EITI Implementation in Nigeria.*
48. Ilda Lindell, *Transnational Activism Networks and Gendered Gatekeeping. Negotiating Gender in an African Association of Informal Workers.*

2012

49. Terje Oestigaard, *Water Scarcity and Food Security along the Nile. Politics, population increase and climate change.*
50. David Ross Olanya, *From Global Land Grabbing for Biofuels to Acquisitions of AfricanWater for Commercial Agriculture.*

2013

51. Gessesse Dessie, *Favouring a Demonised Plant. Khat and Ethiopian smallholder enterprise.*
52. Boima Tucker, *Musical Violence. Gangsta Rap and Politics in Sierra Leone.*
53. David Nilsson, *Sweden-Norway at the Berlin Conference 1884–85. History, national identity-making and Sweden's relations with Africa.*

54. Pamela K. Mbabazi, *The Oil Industry in Uganda; A Blessing in Disquise or an all Too Familiar Curse? Paper presented at the Claude Ake Memorial Lecture.*
55. Måns Fellesson & Paula Mählck, *Academics on the Move. Mobility and Institutional Change in the Swedish Development Support to Research Capacity Buildiing in Mozambique.*
56. Clementina Amankwaah. *Election-Related Violence: The Case of Ghana.*

2014

57. Farida Mahgoub. *Current Status of Agriculture and Future Challenges in Sudan.*
58. Emy Lindberg. *Youth and the Labour Market in Liberia – on history, state structures and spheres of informalities.*
59. Marianna Wallin. *Resettled for Development. The Case of New Halfa Agricultural Scheme, Sudan.*

2015

60. Joseph Watuleke. *The Role of Food Banks in Food Security in Uganda. The Case of the Hunger Project Food Bank, Mbale Epicentre.*
61. Victor A.O. Adetula. *African Conflicts, Development and Regional Organisations in the Post-Cold War International System. The Annual Claude Ake Memoral Lecture Uppsala, Sweden 30 January 2014.*
62. Terje Oestigaard. *Dammed Divinities. The Water Powers at Bujagali Falls, Uganda.*
63. Atakilte Beyene. *Agricultural Water in East Africa.*

www.ingramcontent.com/pod-product-compliance
Ingram Content Group UK Ltd.
Pitfield, Milton Keynes, MK11 3LW, UK
UKHW051351180426
11947UKWH00014B/870